THE DESIGN AND CONSTRUCTION OF DEADLOCK-FREE CONCURRENT SYSTEMS

Jeremy Malcolm Randolph Martin

Thesis submitted for the degree of D.Phil. to the School of Sciences
at the University of Buckingham in 1996

ABSTRACT
THE DESIGN AND CONSTRUCTION OF DEADLOCK-FREE CONCURRENT SYSTEMS

Jeremy Martin

It is a difficult task to produce software that is guaranteed never to fail, but it is a vital goal for which to strive in many real-life situations. The problem is especially complex in the field of parallel programming, where there are extra things that can go wrong. A particularly serious problem is deadlock. Here, we consider how to construct systems that are guaranteed deadlock-free by design.

Design rules, old and new, that eliminate deadlock are catalogued and their theoretical foundation illuminated. Then the development of a software engineering tool is described, which proves deadlock freedom by verifying adherence to these methods. The use of this tool is illustrated with several case studies.

The thesis concludes with a discussion of related issues of parallel program reliability.

ACKNOWLEDGEMENTS

I am indebted to my supervisors, Ian East and Sabah Jassim, for their guidance, encouragement, and enthusiasm for science. I have also greatly benefited from discussions with their former colleague, John Rowe. My thesis is based largely on the previous work and ideas of Bill Roscoe and Peter Welch, both of whom have been very helpful.

I am very grateful to my sister, Clare, who originally suggested to me the idea of studying for a doctorate and put me in touch with my supervisors. She also provided me with a lot of useful background material. The University of Buckingham has proved to be a very pleasant environment to work in, with excellent facilities. I must also thank my employers, Oxford University Computing Services, for giving me time off to study.

Many thanks are due to my wife, Nathalie, who often found that although my body was present, my mind was elsewhere. Thanks also to my children Adrian, Alex (who popped up half way through), and Clarisse (who popped up right at the end) for all the fun that we have had.

This thesis is dedicated, with love, to the memory of Phyllis Amy Martin, 1906–1994.

CONTENTS

LIST OF FIGURES

LIST OF TABLES

DECLARATION

I would like to draw attention to the following material contained within this thesis, which I believe to be original.

Chapter 2: Theorems 7 and 9 are new results that generalise a theorem of A. W. Roscoe and N. Dathi and several theorems of P. H. Welch. Theorem 7 forms part of a joint publication:

J. Martin, I. East, and S. Jassim. *Design Rules for Deadlock-Freedom*, Transputer Communications, September 1994.

The definition of the Client-Server Protocol, and the results which follow, are a new formal adaptation of informal ideas due to Welch, G. R. R. Justo, and C. J. Willcock. The Extended Resource Allocation Protocol (Rule 11) is also new.

Chapter 3: Apart from the section that describes the normalisation of transition systems, this chapter is based entirely on original work.

Chapter 4: The first two case studies considered are original implementations of the existing algorithms. The third is an original analysis of a published algorithm that reveals a deficiency and proposes a solution to this problem.

To the best of my knowledge, none of this material has ever previously been submitted for a degree at this or any other university.

PREFACE

Dear Reader,

It is now thirty years since I started my doctoral studies at the University of Buckingham in the field of Computer Science and specifically the phenomenon of Deadlock. At that time, I was working as a computer programmer at Oxford University Computing Services. I had previously studied for a degree in Mathematics, and I relished the opportunity of getting into postgraduate studies part time while still working in an interesting field and, in particular, to understand a lot more about Formal Methods that could be used to apply Mathematics to solving problems in Computing, thus linking my two main interests together.

I had two excellent supervisors at Buckingham: Ian East, Astrophysicist turned Computer Scientist, and Sabah Jassim, Algebraic Topologist. The research project had been defined by Ian. It concerned the difficulties of building computer systems from separate component processes which run concurrently and communicate with each other and being sure to avoid the potentially catastrophic problem of Deadlock.

Deadlock is a phenomenon specific to a concurrent system where none of its components can agree with each other upon what to do next and the whole system therefore halts. Computer professionals have been creating concurrent systems for at least sixty years and this problem has recurred frequently and has continued to pose a threat to the success of projects and to the operation of safety critical systems up to the present day. The main aim of my doctoral project was to precisely define a catalogue of design rules that engineers could use to ensure that the concurrent systems they were building would never suffer from deadlock and also to carry out mathematical proofs to show that these design rules were indeed robust. Plenty of work had been done in this area previously, notably by Professors Bill Roscoe of the Oxford University and Peter Welch of the University of Kent. Roscoe had been one of the architects of the CSP (Communicating Sequential Processes) algebra for defining and describing concurrent systems, along with Stephen Brookes and its original inventor Tony Hoare [Brookes and Roscoe 2021].

As an example, let us consider the following *informal* design rule for Deadlock Freedom, the Resource Allocation Protocol.

> *Suppose we have a collection of concurrent processes which may each periodically acquire and then release shared resources from a numbered set. The system will be deadlock free if no process ever attempts to acquire a higher-numbered resource than any that it already holds*[1].

This rule could be useful for allocation of computer memory to running processes in an operating system, or for locking data items for updates in a relational database. But it might also create performance limitations in certain situations.

In my thesis I provide formal definitions of existing informal rules including the Resource Allocation Protocol, and mathematical justifications for their correctness, using the CSP process algebra. I also derive generalisations and combinations of these rules to build a comprehensive portfolio of easy-to-follow principles for guaranteeing deadlock freedom of complex concurrent systems by design. This is supported by a collection of realistic industrial-scale case studies.

A secondary phase of my doctoral project was to create an automated verification tool, the Deadlock Checker [Martin 1997, Martin and Jassim 1997b, Martin and Jassim 1997c]. It works in two ways: *either* by checking for rigid adherence to specific design patterns *or* by applying a graph theoretical algorithm which I discovered and called the *State Dependence Digraph* [Martin and Jassim 1997a].

The State Dependence Digraph of a concurrent system is a defined as a digraph where each vertex corresponds to a state of an individual process, and each arc represents a potential 'ungranted' request to communicate from one process to another. It is constructed by local analysis of each subnetwork of pairs of processes – so avoids any enumeration of global states of the system. It is shown that if the state dependence digraph is circuit-free, then there can never be a cycle of ungranted requests, which implies that the network is deadlock-free.

---

[1]Note that the informal statement of this rule given here is over-simplified, and there are a few other conditions that need to be satisfied, such as non-termination of the individual processes and there being no other communication apart from acquiring and releasing resources.

This is shown to be able to prove many useful networks deadlock-free, going beyond the bounds of the design rules.

Figure 0.1: Example of a State Dependence Digraph with Four Processes

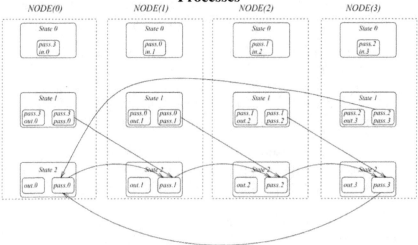

This novel approach was very efficient and therefore able to prove deadlock freedom for arbitrarily large networks of processes. It made use of the compilation feature from the CSP refinement checking tool FDR (Failures Divergence Refinement) [Gibson-Robinson *et al* 2017] to convert CSP notation into process flows. FDR itself is capable of proving deadlock freedom but suffers from the phenomenon of exponential global state explosion as the number of processes within a system grows. It provides a complete method for checking deadlock freedom for finite state concurrent systems but works by exhaustively checking every global state, and hence is only suitable for proving deadlock freedom for very small systems. On the other hand, the Deadlock Checker's SDD algorithm is not complete - it cannot prove deadlock freedom for every deadlock free system, but it works with high efficiency in terms of the number of constituent processes because its works predominantly through local analysis of pair of processes within the system.

In summary, the upshot of all this work was to provide:

1. A comprehensive suite of design rules for constructing elegant concurrent systems which are guaranteed never to deadlock,
2. A mathematical justification of the correctness of these rules,
3. A proof tool for verifying that specific systems meet these rules which works on very large numbers of processes,

4. An illustration of the benefits of these contributions with some industrial scale case studies.

So how is this work still relevant today? Firstly, the CSP mathematical notation is just as valid today as it was 30 years ago. It has not changed, and this continues to be used in many high profile areas, such as Defence, Cyber Security and Reliable Software Engineering [Brookes and Roscoe 2021]. CSP research was instrumental in the development of Transputer processors and the Occam programming language, both of which were widely used at the time of my doctoral research. These technologies are less mainstream today but, fortunately, CSP process algebra is agnostic to the actual programming languages and hardware being used and subsequent work has provided CSP communication libraries for Java [Welch and Martin 2004] and Python, two of our most popular coding languages today. There is also a new and successful programming language, Go, which directly incorporates the CSP model. And use of concurrency in computer systems has continued to grow, for instance with the widespread use of the Microservices Architecture [Martin and Boggis 2018] and adoption of Cloud Computing [Martin and Tiskin 2004, Martin *et al* 2009], which means that the deadlock problem potentially looms larger than ever.

I am also pleased to report that there has been a follow-up doctoral project in the specific area of proving deadlock-freedom completed by Pedro Antonino, under the supervision of Roscoe. In their publication with Thomas Gibson-Robinson, *Efficient deadlock-freedom checking using local analysis and sat solving* [Antonino *et al* 2016], they state:

> "Our work has been inspired by Martin's definition of the State Dependency Digraph. We regard our framework as a development on the SDD. Martin's analysis of SDDs is one of the most general prior approaches to local deadlock analysis."

The work considers the concept of the 'pairwise-reachable' global states of the system. These might not all actually be *reachable* states. So it sits between the set of reachable states and the cartesian product of all the states of each individual process. Examination of pairwise-reachable states is enabled by expressing the deadlock freedom condition as a Boolean satisfiability problem and applying a 'SAT solver' tool to attempt to evaluate the condition[2].

---

[2] A SAT solver is a computer program which aims to solve the Boolean satisfiability problem. On input a formula over Boolean variables, such as "(x or y) and (x or not y)", a SAT solver outputs whether the formula is satisfiable, meaning that there are possible values of x and y which make the formula true, or unsatisfiable, meaning that there are no such values of x and y."

The authors show that their algorithm, called 'Pair', is at least 'as good as' SDD – it can prove deadlock freedom for a system whenever SDD can. However, the flip side of this is that it is not guaranteed to execute efficiently, unlike SDD. Pair is more applicable than SDD but less scalable. This work is further developed in a separate paper from the same authors, introducing some enhancements to add extra information into the Pair algorithm regarding global invariants, which is akin to my development of the SDD into 'coloured' versions of the digraph covered in my thesis [Antonino et al 2017].

It is worth mentioning here, as noted by Antonino et al, that many safety properties of Concurrent Systems beyond deadlock can be reduced to verifying deadlock freedom of modified systems, which increases the potential applicability of my work and theirs [Godefroid and Wolper 1993].

At the end of my thesis, which was completed in 1996, I made a prediction for the future that we would soon see an integrated development environment for both the abstract CSP language and actual programming languages that would incorporate automated proof tools in the style of FDR and Deadlock Checker. This has now come to pass in several ways. There are now a number of domain-specific languages for which translators to CSP exist – allowing FDR checks to be directly applied to the resultant code. The first of these was the hugely-successful Casper language that was created by Lowe for analysing and attempting to crack cryptographic protocols [Lowe 1996], [Lowe 1999], [Ryan et al 2001]. More recently, the father-and-daughter team of Broadfoot and Hopcroft, identified the possibility of combining CSP and FDR and existing software engineering approaches to create a compositional approach to the development of embedded control systems [Broadfoot and Hopcroft 2005] with considerable success and adoption by a number of large companies. This has in turn recently led to the development of a new programming language, Coco, designed for event-driven software and a model checker Cosmos designed to check Coco programs via translation to CSP by Hopcroft and Gibson-Robinson, supported by the Cocotec company. As regards integrated development environments and code analysis tools, there has been massive uptake and ever-increasing functionality, of products such as Eclipse [Burnette 2005] and SonarQube [Gaudin and Mallet 2010] to help drive the DevSecOps transformation of Systems Engineering. However there are still many organisations that seem to be stuck in the old ways of working, seemingly with a high level of tolerance of defects with most of the effort to remediate these being driven by testing and monitoring rather than striving to eliminate defects at the design stage before any code is written.

Carrying out my doctoral studies at Buckingham has led to some interesting changes of direction in my career. Shortly after completing my project, I secured a role in the brand new Oxford Supercomputing Centre as Parallel Computing Advisor for a consortium of scientific departments. To expand my knowledge of High Performance Computing technology, I engaged upon a personal project to adapt the FDR/CSP model checking algorithms to work across many parallel processors [Martin and Huddart 2000] and was able to demonstrate a remarkable linear speed up of this calculation compared with the conventional desktop FDR software. I used a simple hashing technique to distributed global states of the system uniformly between processors. Off the back of this work I was engaged as a consultant by Formal Systems Europe, the company which developed and marketed FDR at that time, to build the first parallelised version of their product running on a Linux server cluster and using the MPI high performance computing message passing library, with similar success [Goldsmith and Martin 2002]. This provided the blueprint for future versions of the FDR software which has been shown to run on a cloud installation of 1024 processes with super-linear speed up (which means that it runs more than 1024 times faster than it does in a single machine) [Gibson-Robinson *et al* 2017]. My involvement in high performance computing at Oxford led me to become interested in Human Genetics and I subsequently worked for a startup biotechnology company that spun out from the University for five years doing some fascinating research-related computing. From there I moved into the Pharmaceutical Domain where my main role was to run a High Performance Computing service, helping to drive forward drug discovery and strategies for vaccination programmes. I then moved on to the Lloyds of London Insurance Market to lead the team programming and running mathematical simulations of the entire global insurance business using powerful HPC technology. I have also retained my interest in Computer Science research and continue to publish papers and attend conferences. In 2021 I was able to use the FDR tool to analyse and fix a problem that I had seen in the insurance world where an automated claims payment system contained a bug that would lead to a claim potentially being paid twice because of a race condition [Martin 2021].

There have been some very significant areas where concurrency theory and in particular CSP have proved to be invaluable over the past thirty years. As already mentioned, one of these has been in cyber security and verifying or cracking cryptography protocols. Work by Lowe and Roscoe has led to virtually every published cryptographic protocol having been cracked and this was achieved using the FDR tool by simulating a wiretapper spying on messages between two parties and inserting spoof messages in order to discover secrets [Ryan *et al* 2001]. Another important area of development has been to implement CSP message passing libraries for commonly used programming languages such as Java and Python. But how do we know that these implementations correctly implement the CSP model and can be trusted to behave in a way that can be modelled and analysed within CSP model checker FDR? I collaborated with Peter Welch to develop a CSP model for his Java CSP implementation JCSP [Welch and Martin 2004]. We wanted to prove that the channels in that Java library would behave in the same way as CSP channels with respect to problems such as deadlock and overall process correctness. The proof we constructed for this was interesting because it required a hybrid combination of automation and algebra, in order for our proof to scale up to arbitrarily large networks of processes containing many instances of the JCSP channel. One of the limitations of FDR is that it can only be applied to finite state processes (with a few exceptions). To prove general theorems about process networks typically requires an algebraic proof using the CSP mathematical model directly and taking advantage of the algebraic laws of CSP that have been derived from that model. Welch and I were able to farm out some of the heavy lifting to the FDR tool as part of our algebraic proof of the correctness of the JCSP channel implementation.

Above I described how I had applied High Performance Computing technology to scale up automated verification of properties in concurrent systems based on the CSP process algebra, and how this approach was integrated into the FDR model checker which has been shown to scale up to run efficiently run on a grid of over one thousand processors. More recently I have returned the favour by applying Formal Methods to High Performance Computing. I came up with the idea of applying the principle of Data Refinement to Parallel Scientific Computing. Essentially I treat a distributed parallel program with its data partitioned across multiple systems as being a *concrete* refinement of an *abstract* scientific algorithm, and explain how to utilise the technique of *coupling invariants* to prove the correctness of the parallel algorithm [Martin 2018].

When I wrote my thesis, there was a lack of any textbook which explained the CSP framework as it stood at the time and, as already mentioned, still stands today. I hoped that my volume would act as a useful primer for people getting into this field, since the only up-to-date documentation available at the time of its completion was spread across various papers published by Roscoe, Brookes and their collaborators. The famous volume, *Communicating Sequential Processes*, written by Tony Hoare [Hoare 1985] remained a great source of inspiration, but it described an earlier dialect and mathematical model which had been somewhat superseded by his doctoral students' work, those students having been Roscoe and Brooks. We now have two advanced textbooks from Roscoe which cover the subject in far more detail [Roscoe 1998, Roscoe 2010], but I believe my thesis still stands as a good introduction to the problem of managing concurrency, and the CSP language as it is used today.

Recently I was asked to present a keynote address at the 2023 Concurrent Processes Architectures and Embedded Systems Conference. My talk was entitled *Concurrency and Models of Abstraction: Past, Present and Future* and I presented a personal view of the most successful abstract patterns for concurrency of the last sixty years [Martin 2023]. Of course, the CSP process algebra was one of these, but I also included some very well-known patterns that are sometimes taken for granted due to our familiarity with them, but on reflection seem to have been huge enablers for major technical advances and efficiencies from which we benefit today. For instance, I argued that the successful development and evolution of the Internet owes a great detail to the simple four layer pattern used for the Internet Protocol Stack, which resembles the Client-Server design pattern explored within my thesis.

Finally, I would like to share with you with the following quotation from Tony Hoare, as relayed by Brookes and Roscoe [Brookes and Roscoe 2021].

> "*In the development of the understanding of complex phenomena, the most powerful tool available to the human intellect is abstraction. Abstraction arises from the recognition of similarities between certain objects, situations, or processes in the real world and the decision to concentrate on these similarities and to ignore, for the time being, their differences.*"

I hope you will enjoy reading this!
Jeremy Martin, London 2023.

REFERENCES

[Antonino *et al* 2016] Pedro Antonino, Thomas Gibson-Robinson, and A.W. Roscoe *Efficient deadlock-freedom checking using local analysis and sat solving*, in International Conference on Integrated Formal Methods, pages 345–360. Springer, 2016.

[Antonino *et al* 2017] Pedro Antonino, Thomas Gibson-Robinson, and A.W. Roscoe *The automatic detection of token structures and invariants using sat checking*, in International Conference on Tools and Algorithms for the Construction and Analysis of Systems, pages 249–265. Springer, 2017.

[Burnette 2005] Ed Burnett *Eclipse IDE Pocket Guide: Using the Full-Featured IDE,* O'Reilly Media 2005.

[Broadfoot and Hopcroft 2005] Guy H Broadfoot and PJ Hopcroft *Introducing formal methods into industry using cleanroom and CSP*, Dedicated Systems Magazine, 2005.

[Brookes and Roscoe 2021] Brookes, Stephen D., and A. W. Roscoe *CSP: A practical process algebra*, Theories of Programming: The Life and Works of Tony Hoare. 2021. 187–222.

[Gibson-Robinson *et al* 2017] Thomas Gibson-Robinson, Guy Broadfoot, Gustavo Carvalho, Philippa Hopcroft, Gavin Lowe, Sidney Nogueira, Colin O'Halloran, and Augusto Sampaio *FDR: from theory to industrial application*, In Concurrency, Security, and Puzzles, pages 65–87. Springer, 2017.

[Gaudin and Mallet 2010] Olivier Gaudin and Freddy Mallet *Sonar*, Methods and Tools Vol. 18, no. 1. 2010-03-01. pp. 40–46. ISSN 1661-402X 2010.

[Godefroid and Wolper 1993] Patrice Godefroid and Pierre Wolper. *Using partial orders for the efficient verification of deadlock freedom and safety properties*, FMSD, 2(2):149–164, 1993.

[Goldsmith and Martin 2002] M. Goldsmith and J. Martin *Parallelization of FDR,* in Workshop on Parallel and Distributed Model Checking, affiliated to CONCUR 2002 (13th International Conference on Concurrency Theory), Brno, Czech Republic 2002.

[Hoare 1985] C. A. R. Hoare Communicating Sequential Processes, Prentice-Hall 1985.

[Lowe 1996] Gavin Lowe *Breaking and fixing the Needham-Schroeder public-key protocol using FDR*, in International Workshop on Tools and Algorithms for the Construction and Analysis of Systems, pages 147–166. Springer, 1996. 29.

[Lowe 1999] Gavin Lowe *Casper: A compiler for the analysis of security protocols*, Journal of computer security, 6(1-2):53–84, 1998.

[Martin 1997] J. M. R. Martin *Deadlock Checker: Documentation and Download Site,* http://wotug.org/parallel/theory/formal/csp/Deadlock/ 1997.

[Martin 2000] J. M. R. Martin *A tool for checking the CSP sat property,* Computer Journal Volume 43, Number 1, 2000.

[Martin 2018] Jeremy M. R. Martin *Testing and Verifying Parallel Programs Using Data Refinement,* Proceedings of Communicating Process Architecture 2018, IOS Press.

[Martin 2021] Jeremy M. R. Martin *Designing and Verifying Microservices Using CSP,* Proceedings of 2021 IEEE Concurrent Processes Architectures and Embedded Systems Virtual Conference (COPA 2021).

[Martin 2023] Jeremy M. R. Martin *Concurrency and Models of Abstraction: Past, Present and Future,* To appear in proceedings of 2023 IEEE Concurrent Processes Architectures and Embedded Systems Virtual Conference (COPA 2023).

[Martin and Boggis 2018] Jeremy M. R. Martin and Peter J Boggis *Use Case Driven Microservices Architecture Design,* Proceedings of Communicating Process Architecture 2018, IOS Press 2018.

[Martin and Huddart 2000] J. M. R. Martin and Y Huddart *Parallel Algorithms for Deadlock and Livelock Analysis of Concurrent Systems,* Proceedings of Communicating Process Architecture 2000, IOS Press 2000.

[Martin and Jassim 1997a] J. Martin, and S. Jassim *A Tool for Proving Deadlock Freedom, in Parallel Programming and Java,* Proceedings of the 20th World Occam and Transputer User Group Technical Meeting, IOS Press 1997.

[Martin and Jassim 1997b] J. Martin, and S. Jassim *How to Design Deadlock-Free Networks Using CSP and Verilication Tools-A Tutorial Introduction,* in Parallel Programming and Java, Proceedings of the 20th World Occam and Transputer User Group Technical Meeting, IOS Press 1997.

[Martin and Jassim 1997c] J. Martin and S. Jassim *An Efficient Technique for Deadlock Analysis of Large Scale Process Networks*, Proceedings of the Formal Methods Europe '97 International Symposium, Springer-Verlag LNCS 1997.

[Martin and Tiskin 2004] Jeremy M. R. Martin and Alexander V. Tiskin *Dynamic BSP: Towards a Flexible Approach to Parallel Computing over the Grid*, Proceedings of Communicating Process Architecture 2004, IOS Press 2004.

[Martin *et al* 2009] Jeremy M. R. Martin, Steven J. Barrett, Simon J. Thornber, Silviu-Alin Bacanu, Dale Dunlap, Steve Weston *Economics of Cloud Computing: a Statistical Genetics Case Study*, Proceedings of Communicating Process Architecture 2009, IOS Press 2009.

[Roscoe 1998] A. W. Roscoe *The theory and practice of concurrency*, Prentice Hall. 1998.

[Roscoe 2010] A.W. Roscoe *Understanding Concurrent Systems*, Springer. 2010.

[Ryan *et al* 2001] Peter Ryan, Steve A Schneider, Michael Goldsmith, Gavin Lowe, and A.W. Roscoe *The modelling and analysis of security protocols: the CSP approach*, Addison-Wesley Professional, 2001.

[Welch and Martin 2004] P. H. Welch and J. M. R. Martin *A CSP Model for Java Multithreading*, Proceedings of the International Symposium on Software Engineering for Parallel and Distributed Systems (PDSE 2000), IEEE Press 2000.

INTRODUCTION

THE DEADLOCK PROBLEM

Throughout our lives, we take for granted the safety of complex structures that surround us. We live and work in buildings with scant regard for the lethal currents of electricity and flammable gas coarsing through their veins. We cross high bridges with little fear of them crumbling into the depths below. We are secure in the knowledge that these objects have been constructed using sound engineering principles.

Now, increasingly, we are putting our lives in the hands of complex computer programs. One could cite aircraft control systems, railway signalling systems, and medical databases as examples. Although the disciplines of electrical and mechanical engineering have long been well understood, software engineering is in its infancy. Unlike other fields, there is no generally accepted certification of competence for its practitioners.

Formal scientific methods for reliable software production have been developed, but these tend to require a level of mathematical knowledge beyond that of most programmers. Engineers, in general, are usually more concerned with practical issues than with the underlying scientific theory of their particular discipline. They want to get on with the business of building powerful systems. They rely on scientists to provide them with safety rules that they can incorporate into their designs. For instance, a bridge designer needs to know certain formulae to calculate how wide to set the span of an arch; he does not need to know *why* the formulae work. Software engineering is in need of a battery of similar rules to provide a bridge between theory and practice.

The demand for increasing amounts of computing power makes parallel programming very appealing. However, additional dangers lurk in this exciting field. In this thesis, we explore ways to circumvent one particularly dramatic problem – deadlock. This is a state where none of the constituent processes of a system can agree on how to proceed, so nothing ever happens. Clearly, we would desire that any sensible system we construct could never arrive at such a state, but what can we do to ensure that this is indeed the case?

We might think to use a computer to check every possible state of the system. But, given that the number of states in a parallel system usually grows exponentially with the number of processes, we would most likely find the task too great. Perhaps we would conduct experimental tests to try to induce deadlock. This approach would reveal any obvious problems, but there might be deadlocks that require many years of running time to appear, which we would never detect. We could attempt to construct a mathematical proof of deadlock freedom, but we would soon discover that, even for small programs, this is often extremely difficult and time-consuming. The problem with all these approaches is that the deadlock issue has been left to the end of the software development process, when it is really too late. Design rules are needed, which may be applied *á priori*: rules that guarantee deadlock freedom, are not too restrictive, and are easy to follow.

Early work in concurrency was framed in the context of multitasking operating systems. The idea was to share an expensive collection of hardware resources between a number of user processes. The classic illustration of the risk of deadlock in this situation is the Dining Philosophers of E. W. Dijkstra (described in [Hoare 1985]).

Five philosophers sit around a table. Each has a fork to his left. An everlasting bowl of spaghetti is placed in the middle of the table. A philosopher spends most of his time thinking, but whenever he is hungry, he picks up the fork to his left and plunges it into the bowl. As the spaghetti is very long and tangled, he requires another fork to carry it to his mouth, so he picks up the fork to his right as well. If, on attempting to pick up either fork, he should find that it is already in use, he simply waits until it becomes available again. When he has finished eating, he puts down both forks and continues to think.

There is a serious flaw in this system, which is only revealed when all the philosophers become hungry at the same time. They each pick up their left-hand fork and then reach out for their right-hand fork, which is not there – a clear case of deadlock.

Figure 0.2: Deadlocked Dining Philosophers

Rules of varying complexity have been devised to tackle this problem. The simplest is to allocate to each resource a unique integer priority. Then deadlock may be avoided by ensuring that no user process ever tries to acquire a resource with a higher priority than one it already holds. In the case of the Dining Philosophers, we could label the forks from zero to four, clockwise around the table. Four out of the five philosophers would then have a fork of higher priority to their left than their right, and so their behaviour would conform to the rule. The fifth, however, would have fork number zero to his left and fork number four to his right, so he would break the rule. If he were to modify his behaviour to always pick up the fork to his right first, the risk of deadlock would be removed. This example illustrates the power of using design rules to prevent pathological behaviour. The theory behind this particular rule is described in Chapter 2.

As computer hardware becomes more abundant, the main issue in concurrency is no longer how to share out sparse resources between multiple tasks but rather how best to spread a single task over multiple resources in order to improve performance. Here, a task is decomposed into processes that communicate with each other, and it is these communications that pose the threat of deadlock. Concurrent programming languages provide little safeguard against this demon. Deadlock is also a potential hazard in naturally distributed systems, such as telephone networks and control programs for complex machines. Imagine a control program for the cooling system of a nuclear reactor. The program might run smoothly for many years without problem. Unless rigorous methods had been used throughout to guarantee that the program was free from deadlock, there would be no way of knowing for sure whether a particular set of conditions could one day arise that would cause it to deadlock, perhaps resulting in meltdown.

SUMMARY

The intention of this thesis is to provide a rigorous means of engineering deadlock-free concurrent systems of arbitrary size. The approach taken is to provide a collection of design rules that may be used to guarantee freedom from deadlock. These rules are by no means *complete*, but they do offer sufficient flexibility to be applicable to a wide range of problems. A welcome bonus is that their use often leads to algorithms that are more structured and elegant than those developed by 'trial and error'.

Most programmers are, to some extent, error-prone. With this in mind, a tool has been developed to check for conformance to the design rules. It will be shown how the combined weapons of design rules and automatic verification provide a vital defence against the patient and cunning foe that is deadlock.

Chapter 1 outlines the algebraic language of communicating sequential processes (CSP), which is used for specifying systems of communicating processes. A summary of the existing techniques for deadlock analysis using this model is provided.

Chapter 2 introduces some design rules for avoiding deadlock. These are formalised in CSP. It is shown how they may be generalised and combined to provide a coherent strategy for the design of deadlock-free systems.

Chapter 3 describes the development of a software engineering tool for deadlock analysis: Deadlock Checker. This is based on the results of the preceding chapters.

Chapter 4 comprises several interesting case studies of constructing deadlock-free concurrent systems with the occam programming language using design rules.

We conclude with a discussion of how the design approach might be extended to a wider domain of correctness issues.

A certain amount of mathematical terminology and notation is employed, deriving from Set Theory and Logic, Partial Orders, and Graph Theory. In the interests of self-containment and also due to a lack of consistency in the literature, the basics of the latter two fields are summarised in Appendices A and B.

1

COMMUNICATING SEQUENTIAL PROCESSES AND DEADLOCK

INTRODUCTION

This chapter is concerned with laying the mathematical foundations for the thesis. To construct rigorous design rules for program design, we must first define a programming environment. This chapter introduces the CSP language of C.A.R. Hoare, which stands for *Communicating Sequential Processes* [Hoare 1985]. It is a notation for describing patterns of communication through algebraic expressions. These may be manipulated and transformed according to various laws in order to establish important properties of the system being described.

Behind CSP lies a mathematical theory of *failures* and *divergences*. Here, a process is defined in terms of abstract sets representing circumstances under which it might be observed to go wrong. The model supplies a precise mathematical meaning to CSP processes and is consistent with the algebraic laws that govern them.

The standard operational model of CSP is also described. Here, the processes are represented by transition systems, which illustrate their inner machinery. There is a close relationship between the operational model of CSP and the Failures-Divergences model, which means that the former may be used to prove properties of a system phrased in terms of the latter.

Following this, the concept of deadlock is formalised, and we introduce techniques for deadlock analysis developed by S.D. Brookes, A.W. Roscoe, and N. Dathi. The problem of livelock is also considered.

CSP is not a programming language strictly speaking; it is a mathematical notation. However, there are a number of concurrent programming languages based on CSP, such as occam and Ada, so the theoretical results derived using this model are applicable to real programming.

1.1 THE CSP LANGUAGE

The basic syntax of CSP is described by the following grammar

$$
\begin{aligned}
Process \ ::== \ & STOP \mid \\
& SKIP \mid \\
& event \ \rightarrow \ Process \mid \\
& Process \, ; Process \mid \\
& Process \mid [alph \mid alph] \mid Process \mid \\
& Process \parallel\mid Process \mid \\
& Process \ \sqcap \ Process \mid \\
& Process \ \square \ Process \mid \\
& Process \backslash event \mid \\
& f(Process) \mid \\
& name \mid \\
& \mu \ name \ \bullet \ Process
\end{aligned}
$$

Here, *event* ranges over a universal set of events, Σ, *alph* ranges over subsets of Σ, f ranges over a set of function names, and *name* ranges over a set of process names.

A process describes the behaviour of an object in terms of the events in which it may engage. The simplest process of all is *STOP*. This is the process that represents a deadlocked object. It never engages in any event. Another primitive process is *SKIP*, which does nothing but terminate successfully; it only performs the special event $\checkmark$, which represents successful termination.

An event may be combined with a process using the prefix operator, written $\rightarrow$. The process *bang* $\rightarrow$ *UNIVERSE* describes an object that first engages in event *bang* and then behaves according to process *UNIVERSE*. If we want to give this new process the name *CREATION*, we write this as an equation

$$CREATION \ = \ bang \ \rightarrow \ UNIVERSE$$

Processes may be defined in terms of themselves using the principle of recursion. Consider a process to describe the ticking of an everlasting clock.

$$CLOCK = tick \rightarrow CLOCK$$

CLOCK is a process that performs an event *tick* and then starts again. (This is a somewhat abstract definition. No information is given as to the duration or frequency of ticks. We are simply told that the clock will keep on ticking.)

In an algebraic sense, *CLOCK* has been defined as the solution to an equation of the form

$$X = F(X)$$

It is not always the case in mathematics that such equations have solutions (*e.g.*, there is no real solution to $x = x^2 + x + 1$). Fortunately, the underlying mathematical theory of CSP guarantees that solutions exist to all such equations. The reason for this will be explained later. The solution to $X = F(X)$ is written as

$$\mu Y \bullet F(Y)$$

where Y is a dummy process variable. Using this notation we could write *CLOCK* as

$$\mu Y \bullet tick \rightarrow Y$$

The recursive notation is commonly extended to a set of simultaneous equations where a number of processes are defined in terms of each other. This is known as mutual recursion, several examples of which will be found in later chapters.

There are a number of CSP operations that combine two processes to produce a new one. The first of these that we shall consider is sequential composition.

$$UNIVERSE = EXPAND; CONTRACT$$

is the process that first behaves like *EXPAND*, but when *EXPAND* is ready to terminate, it continues by behaving like *CONTRACT*. However, it may also be possible that *EXPAND* will never terminate.

It is rather more complicated to compose two processes in parallel than in sequence. It is necessary to specify a set of events for each process, known as its *alphabet*. The process denoted

$$\begin{array}{c} FRONT \\ PANTOHORSE = |[\{forward, backward, nod\}| \{forward, backward, wag\}]| \\ BACK \end{array}$$

represents the parallel composition of two processes: *FRONT* with alphabet {*forward, backward, nod*} and *BACK* with alphabet {*forward, backward, wag*}. Here, each process behaves according to its own definition, but with the constraint that events that are in the alphabet of both *FRONT* and *BACK*, *i.e., forward* and *backward*, require their simultaneous participation. However, they may progress independently on those events belonging solely to their own alphabet. If a situation were to arise where *FRONT* could only perform event *forward* and *BACK* could only perform event *backward*, then deadlock would have occurred.

Parallel composition may be extended to three or more processes; given a sequence of processes $V = \langle P_1, ..., P_N \rangle$ with corresponding alphabets $\langle A_1, ... , A_N \rangle$, we write their parallel composition as

$$PAR(V) \;=\; \|_{i=1}^{n} (P_i, A_i)$$

Note that it is implicitly assumed that the termination event $\checkmark$ requires the joint participation of each process P_i, whether or not it is included in their process alphabets.

An alternative form of parallel composition is *interleaving*, where there is no communication between the component processes. In the parallel combination

$$BRAIN \;||| \; MOUTH$$

the two processes, *BRAIN* and *MOUTH*, progress independently of each other and no cooperation is required on any event, except for $\checkmark$, the termination event. Any other actions that are possible for both processes will only be performed by one process at a time. Interleaving is a commutative and associative operation, and so we may extend the notation to various indexed forms, such as

$$|||_{i=1}^{n} P_n, \quad |||_{x:X} P_x$$

A useful feature of CSP is the ability to describe *non-deterministic* behaviour, which is where a process may operate in an unpredictable manner. The process

$$BUFFER \;=\; TWOPLACE \sqcap THREEPLACE$$

may behave either like process *TWOPLACE* or like process *THREE-PLACE*, but there is no way of telling which in advance. The purpose of the $\sqcap$ operator is to specify concurrent systems in an abstract manner. At the design stage, there is no reason to provide any more detail than is necessary, and, where possible, implementation decisions should be deferred until later.

This operation is known as an *internal choice*. CSP also contains an *external choice* operator $\Box$, which enables the future behaviour of a process to be controlled by other processes running along side it in parallel, which, collectively, we call its *environment*.

The process

$$MW = DEFROST \Box COOK$$

may behave like *DEFROST* or like *COOK*. Its behaviour may be controlled by its environment, provided that this control is exercised at the very first event. If an initial event *button1* is offered by *DEFROST* that is not an initial event of *COOK*, then the environment may coerce *MW* into behaving like *DEFROST* by performing *button1* as its initial event. If, however, the environment were to offer an initial event that is allowed by both *DEFROST* and *COOK*, then the choice between them would be non-deterministic.

Both the choice operators may be extended to indexed forms. We write

$$\Box_{x:A} \; x \; \rightarrow \; P_x$$

to represent the behaviour of an object that offers any event of a set A to its environment. Once some initial event x has been performed, the future behaviour of the object is described by the process P_x. However, the process

$$\sqcap_{x:A} \; x \; \rightarrow \; P_x$$

(where, for technical reasons, A must be finite) offers exactly one event x from A to its environment, the choice being non-deterministic.

Sometimes, it is useful to be able to restrict the definition of a process to a subset of relevant events that it performs. This is done using the hiding operator ($\backslash$). The process

$$CREATION \backslash bang$$

behaves like *CREATION*, except that each occurrence of event *bang* is concealed. Note that it is not permitted to hide event $\checkmark$.

Concealment may introduce nondeterminism into deterministic processes. It may also introduce the phenomenon of *divergence*. This is a drastic situation where a process performs an endless series of hidden actions. Consider, for instance, the process

$$CLOCK \backslash tick$$

which is clearly a divergent process.

It is conventional to extend the notation to $P \backslash A$, where A is a finite set of events.

Finally, let us briefly consider process relabelling. Let f be an *alphabet transformation function* $f : \Sigma \rightarrow \Sigma$, which satisfies the property that only finitely many events may be mapped onto a single event. Then, the process $f(P)$ can perform the event $f(e)$ whenever P can perform event e. As an example, consider a function *new*, which maps *tick* to *tock*. Then, we have

$$new(CLOCK) = tock \rightarrow new(CLOCK)$$

Some important algebraic laws that govern CSP processes are given in Figures 1.1 and 1.2, which vary in complexity. They are taken from [Hoare 1985], [Brookes 1983], and [Brookes and Roscoe 1985a]. (In some cases, the syntax has been modified to conform to the version of CSP described above.) Note that this is not a complete list. The following example illustrates the use of these laws.

Consider a process to describe a vending machine that sells tea for a price of one coin and coffee for two coins.

$$VM = coin \rightarrow ((tea \rightarrow VM) \ \Box \ (coin \rightarrow coffee \rightarrow VM))$$

After inserting a coin, a customer can control the future behaviour of the machine by either inserting another coin or taking a cup of tea.

We now define a process that describes a particular customer who loves tea and is prepared to pay for it. Coffee he will tolerate, but only if it is provided free of charge.

$$TD = (coin \rightarrow tea \rightarrow TD) \ \Box \ (coffee \rightarrow TD)$$

To illustrate the use of algebraic laws to simplify CSP process definitions, consider what happens when the tea drinker tries to use the vending machine. Both processes have the alphabet $\{coin, coffee, tea\}$.

$$SYSTEM = VM \,|[\, \{coin, coffee, tea\} \,|\, \{coin, coffee, tea\,\} \,]| \, TD$$

$$= \left(\begin{array}{c} (coin \rightarrow ((tea \rightarrow VM) \ \square \ (coin \rightarrow coffee \rightarrow VM))) \\ |[\, \{coin, coffee, tea\} \,|\{\, coin, coffee, tea\,\} \,]| \\ ((coin \rightarrow tea \rightarrow TD) \ \square \ (coffee \rightarrow TD)) \end{array} \right)$$

$$= coin \rightarrow \left(\begin{array}{c} ((tea \rightarrow VM) \ \square \ (coin \rightarrow coffee \rightarrow VM)) \\ |[\, \{coin, coffee, tea\,\} \,|\{coin, coffee, tea\,\} \,]| \\ tea \rightarrow TD \end{array} \right)$$

using law 1.22 with $X = \{coin\}$, $Y = \{coin, coffee\}$, $Z = \{coin\}$

$$= coin \rightarrow tea \rightarrow (VM \,|[\{coin, coffee, tea\} \,|\, \{coin, coffee, tea\}]| \, TD)$$

using law 1.22 with $X = \{tea, coin\}$, $Y = \{\, tea \,\}$, $Z = \{\, tea\}$

$$= coin \rightarrow tea \rightarrow SYSTEM$$

The system has been reduced to a very simple, sequential definition. We see that although no coffee will be consumed in this situation, the system will never deadlock.

The account of the CSP language given here is incomplete. Only the core language has been considered with certain 'advanced' operators omitted. The language described corresponds to the modern version of CSP, as given in [Formal Systems 1993], which differs slightly from the language presented in Hoare's book [Hoare 1985].

11

Figure 1.1 – Laws of CSP I

$$SKIP \; ; \; P \; = \; P \; ; \; SKIP \; = \; P \tag{1.1}$$

$$STOP \; ; \; P \; = \; STOP \tag{1.2}$$

$$(P \; ; \; Q) \; ; \; R \; = \; P \; ; (Q \; ; \; R) \tag{1.3}$$

$$(a \; \to \; P) \; ; \; Q \; = \; a \to (P \; ; \; Q) \tag{1.4}$$

$$P \; |[\; A \mid B \;]| \; Q \; = \; Q \; |[\; B \mid A \;]| \; P \tag{1.5}$$

$$P \; |[\; A \mid B \cup C \;]| \; (Q \; |[\; B \mid C \;]| \; R) \; = \; (P \; |[\; A \mid B \;]| \; Q) \; |[\; A \cup B \mid C \;]| \; R \tag{1.6}$$

$$P \; ||| \; Q \; = \; Q \; ||| \; P \tag{1.7}$$

$$P \; ||| \; SKIP \; = \; P \tag{1.8}$$

$$P \; ||| \; (Q \; ||| \; R) \; = \; (P \; ||| \; Q) \; ||| \; R \tag{1.9}$$

$$P \sqcap P \; = \; P \tag{1.10}$$

$$P \sqcap Q \; = \; Q \sqcap P \tag{1.11}$$

$$P \sqcap (Q \sqcap R) \; = \; (P \sqcap Q) \sqcap R \tag{1.12}$$

$$P \square P \; = \; P \tag{1.13}$$

$$P \square Q \; = \; Q \square P \tag{1.14}$$

$$P \square (Q \square R) \; = \; (P \square Q) \square R \tag{1.15}$$

$$P \; |[\; A \mid B \;]| \; (Q \sqcap R) \; = \; (P \; |[\; A \mid B \;]| \; Q) \sqcap (P \; |[\; A \mid B \;]| \; R) \tag{1.16}$$

$$P \square (Q \sqcap R) \; = \; (P \square Q) \sqcap (P \square R) \tag{1.17}$$

$$P \sqcap (Q \square R) \; = \; (P \sqcap Q) \square (P \sqcap R) \tag{1.18}$$

$$(x \; \to \; P) \; \square \; (x \; \to \; Q) \; = \; (x \; \to \; P) \sqcap (x \; \to \; Q)$$
$$= \; x \; \to \; (P \square Q) \tag{1.19}$$

$$P \square STOP = P \tag{1.20}$$

$$\square_{x:\{\}} \; x \to P_x \; = \; STOP \tag{1.21}$$

Figure 1.2 – Laws of CSP II

$$\text{Let } P \;=\; \square_{x:X}\; x \to P_x$$

$$Q \;=\; \square_{y:Y}\; y \to Q_y$$

$$\text{Then, } P\;|[A|B]|\;Q \;=\; \square_{z:Z}\; z \to \left(P_z'\;|[A|B]|\;Q_z'\right)$$

$$\text{where } P_z' \;=\; \begin{cases} P_z & \text{if } z \in X \\ P & \text{otherwise} \end{cases}$$

$$\text{and } Q_z' \;=\; \begin{cases} Q_z & \text{if } z \in Y \\ Q & \text{otherwise} \end{cases}$$

$$\text{and } Z \;=\; (X \cap Y) \cup (X-B) \cup (Y-A)$$

$$\text{assuming } X \subseteq A \quad \text{and } Y \subseteq B \tag{1.22}$$

$$\square_{b:B}\,(b \to P_b)\;|||\;\square_{c:C}\,(c \to Q_c) \;=\; (\square_{b:B}\,(b \to (P_b|||\,\square_{c:C}\,(c \to Q_c))))\;\square$$
$$(\square_{c:C}\,(c \to (Q_c|||\,\square_{b:B}\,(b \to P_c)))) \tag{1.23}$$

$$SKIP\backslash x \;=\; SKIP \tag{1.24}$$

$$STOP\backslash x \;=\; STOP \tag{1.25}$$

$$(P\backslash x)\backslash y \;=\; (P\backslash y)\backslash x \tag{1.26}$$

$$(x \to P)\backslash x \;=\; P\backslash x \tag{1.27}$$

$$(x \to P)\backslash y \;=\; x \to (P\backslash y) \text{ if } x \neq y \tag{1.28}$$

$$(P\;;\;Q)\backslash x \;=\; (P\backslash x\;;\;(Q\backslash x) \tag{1.29}$$

$$(P\;|[A\;|\;B]|\;Q)\backslash x \;=\; P\;|[A\;|\;B\;-\;\{x\}]|\;(Q\backslash x)$$
$$\text{if } x \notin A \tag{1.30}$$

$$(P \sqcap Q)\backslash x \;=\; (P\backslash x) \sqcap (Q\backslash x) \tag{1.31}$$

$$((x \to P)\;\square\;(y \to Q))\,\backslash x \;=\; (P\backslash x) \sqcap ((P\backslash x)\;\square\;(y \to (Q\backslash x)))$$
$$\text{if } x \neq y \tag{1.32}$$

$$f(STOP) \;=\; STOP \tag{1.33}$$

$$f(e \to P) \;=\; f(e) \to f(P) \tag{1.34}$$

$$f(P\;;\;Q) \;=\; f(P)\;;\;f(Q) \text{ if } f^{-1}(\checkmark) \;=\; \{\checkmark\} \tag{1.35}$$

$$f(P\;|||\;Q) \;=\; f(P)\;|||\;f(Q) \tag{1.36}$$

$$f(P\;\square\;Q) \;=\; f(P)\;\square\;f(Q) \tag{1.37}$$

$$f(P \sqcap Q) \;=\; f(P) \sqcap f(Q) \tag{1.38}$$

$$f\left(P\backslash f^{-1}(x)\right) \;=\; f(P)\backslash x \tag{1.39}$$

1.2 THE FAILURES-DIVERGENCES MODEL

In the preceding section, the concept of communicating processes was introduced informally, and the corresponding algebraic laws were stated without mathematical justification. In this section, a precise semantic definition of CSP processes is given from which the laws can be deduced. This is known as the *Failures-Divergences* model. Here, a process is defined in terms of important observable properties: *traces*, *failures*, and *divergences*.

A *trace* of a process P is any finite sequence of events that it may initially perform. For instance

$$\{\langle coffee, coffee, coffee \rangle, \langle coin, tea \rangle\} \subset traces(TD)$$

The following useful operations are defined on traces:

- Catenation: $s ^\frown t$

$$\langle s_1, s_2, ..., s_m \rangle ^\frown \langle t_1, t_2, ..., t_n \rangle = \langle s_1, ..., s_m, t_1, ..., t_n \rangle$$

- Restriction: $s \upharpoonright B$, trace s restricted to elements of set B

    Example: $\langle a, b, c, d, b, d, a \rangle \upharpoonright \{a, b, c\} = \langle a, b, c, b, a \rangle$

- Replication: s^n trace s repeated n times

    Example: $\langle a, b \rangle^2 = \langle a, b, a, b \rangle$

- Count: $s \downarrow x$ number of occurrences of event x in trace s

    Example: $\langle x, y, z, x, x \rangle \downarrow x = 3$

- Length: $|s|$ the length of trace s

    Example: $|\langle a, b, c \rangle| = 3$

- Merging: *merge(s,t)* the set of all possible interleavings of trace s with trace t

    Example: $merge(\langle a, b \rangle, \langle c \rangle) = \{\langle a, b, c \rangle, \langle a, c, b \rangle, \langle c, a, b \rangle\}$

A complication of trace interleaving is that the $\checkmark$ event requires the joint participation of both traces. This means that a trace that contains $\checkmark$ cannot be interleaved with one that does not.

Examples: $merge(\langle a, b, \checkmark \rangle, \langle c, \checkmark \rangle) = \left\{ \begin{array}{l} \langle a, b, c, \checkmark \rangle, \\ \langle a, c, b, \checkmark \rangle, \\ \langle c, a, b, \checkmark \rangle \end{array} \right\}$

$$merge(\langle a, b, \checkmark \rangle, \langle c \rangle) = \{\}$$

The *failures* of a process describe the circumstances under which it might deadlock. Each failure of a process P consists of a pair (s, X) where s is a trace of P and X is a set of events that, if offered to P by its environment after it has performed trace s, might be completely refused. For instance

$$(\langle coin, tea, coin, tea, coin, coin \rangle, \{tea, coin\}) \in failures(VM)$$

This describes a situation where the vending machine *VM* has dispensed two cups of tea and then accepted two coins. At this point, the machine is willing only to dispense coffee. If a user arrives who wants tea and is only prepared to take a cup of tea or to insert another coin, then deadlock will ensue.

The concept of failures is commonly used to write specifications for the behaviour of CSP processes. Consider the following specification:

$$\forall (s, X) : failures(P). \; s \downarrow in > s \downarrow out \implies out \notin X$$

This states that whenever process P has performed the event *in* more often than the event *out*, it must guarantee not to refuse event *out*. This might form part of the overall specification for a buffer.

The *divergences* of a process are a list of the traces after which it might diverge, *e.g.*,

$$\langle \rangle \in divergences(CLOCK \backslash tick)$$

There are several further aspects of notation that are needed in order to define the model, which are as follows. The *Power-Set* of a set A, written as $\mathbf{P}A$, consists of all subsets of A. The *Finite Power-Set* of A, written as $p(A)$, consists of all finite subsets of A. The set of all finite sequences (including $\langle \rangle$) that may be formed from elements of A is written A^*.

The *Failures-Divergences* model is based on a universal set of events Σ. Each CSP process is uniquely defined by a pair of sets

(F, D), corresponding to its *failures* and *divergences*, such that

$$F \subseteq \Sigma^* \times \mathbf{P}\Sigma$$
$$D \subseteq \Sigma^*$$

There are seven axioms that such a pair of sets must satisfy in order to qualify as a process. (Note that there are several versions of these in existence in the literature. This version comes from [Brookes and Roscoe 1985a].)

(1) $(\langle\rangle, \{\}) \in F$

(2) $(s^\frown t, \{\}) \in F \implies (s, \{\}) \in F$

(3) $(s, Y) \in F \wedge X \subseteq Y \implies (s, X) \in F$

(4) $(s, X) \in F \wedge (\forall c \in Y.((s^\frown\langle c\rangle, \{\}) \notin F)) \implies (s, X \cup Y) \in F$

(5) $(\forall Y \in p(X) \cdot (s, Y) \in F) \implies (s, X) \in F$

(6) $s \in D \wedge t \in \Sigma^* \implies s^\frown t \in D$

(7) $s \in D \wedge X \subseteq \Sigma \implies (s, X) \in F$

Putting the first four axioms into words tells us that every process starts off with an empty trace (axiom 1). To perform trace s, it must be able to perform any prefix of s (axiom 2). A subset of a refusal set is also a refusal set (axiom 3). If the process can refuse the events in X and cannot perform any of the events in Y as its next step, then it may also refuse $X \cup Y$ (axiom 4). These are all basic intuitive properties of processes.

Axiom 5 states that a set may be refused if all its finite subsets may be refused. This is to allow for the possibility of Σ being an infinite set without complicating the theory.

Axioms 6 and 7 state that once a process diverges, it may subsequently perform any trace imaginable and will behave in a totally non-deterministic manner. This is a rather harsh treatment of the phenomenon of divergence. If we put our *CLOCK* in a vacuum to hide its ticking, we would not expect such dramatic behaviour. It is, however, a convenient means to make the theory work better based on the assumption that the possibility of divergence is catastrophic (see [Roscoe 1994]).

There is a natural *partial order* (see Appendix A) on the set of all processes given by

$$(F_1, D_1) \sqsubseteq (F_2, D_2) \iff F_1 \supseteq F_2 \wedge D_1 \supseteq D_2$$

The interpretation of this is that process P_1 is worse than P_2 if it can deadlock or diverge whenever P_2 can. This ordering is in fact a *complete partial order*. The bottom, or worst, element $\bot$ represents the process that always diverges, corresponding to the decision to treat this form of behaviour as the least desirable. It is a chaotic process that can do absolutely anything in a totally unpredictable manner. It is defined as follows:

$$\begin{aligned} failures(\bot) &= \Sigma^* \times \mathbf{P}\Sigma \\ divergences(\bot) &= \Sigma^* \end{aligned}$$

The *failures* and *divergences* of the fundamental CSP terms are defined in Figures 1.3 and 1.4. (These are the same as in [Brookes and Roscoe 1985a], except that the definitions of parallel composition and interleaving are modified to reflect the fact that in the modern version of CSP, these operators implicitly require the cooperation of both processes in performing the $\checkmark$ event.) This covers all closed, non-recursive CSP terms.

All of the CSP operators can be shown to be *well-defined*. In other words, if you apply any of them to existing CSP processes, the resulting object will itself be a process: its failures and divergences obeying the seven axioms of the model. They are also *continuous*, with respect to $\sqsubseteq$. This is important because it means that any recursive CSP equation of the form $X = F(X)$ has a solution, by Tarski's fixed point theorem (see Appendix A). The *least* solution is given by

$$\mu X \bullet F(X) = \sqcup \{F^n(\bot)|n \in N\}$$

This means that if you want to find the solution to $X = F(X)$, you start at the bottom $\bot$ and repeatedly apply the function F to it. For instance, *CLOCK* is the limit of the series

$$\bot, tick \rightarrow \bot, tick \rightarrow tick \rightarrow \bot, tick \rightarrow tick \rightarrow tick \rightarrow \bot,..$$

The failures and divergences of $\mu X \bullet F(X)$ may be calculated as follows:

$$\begin{aligned} divergences(\mu X \bullet F(X)) &= \bigcap_{n \in N} divergences\ (F^n(\bot)) \\ failures\ (\mu X \bullet F(X)) &= \bigcap_{n \in N} failures\ (F^n(\bot)) \end{aligned}$$

This is how we define the meaning of recursion in CSP.

This approach may be extended to mutual recursion, where a number of processes are defined by a system of simultaneous equations.

The trick here is to let X be a vector of processes satisfying an equation of the form $X = F(X)$. The solution is then defined as the least fixed point of F in the same way as before.

Whilst the fact that recursion is well-defined in CSP is crucial to the theory, it is really only of technical interest to a designer of concurrent systems. Basically, it allows him to specify processes recursively, assured in the knowledge that it is a sound practice.

The *Failures-Divergences* model of CSP is used for formal reasoning about the behaviour of concurrent systems defined by CSP equations. The partial ordering of nondeterminism is very important for the stepwise refinement of concurrent systems. Starting from an abstract, non-deterministic definition, details of components may be independently fleshed out whilst preserving important properties of the overall system, such as freedom from deadlock. This will be explained in more detail later.

Figure 1.3 – Denotational Semantics for CSP I

$$divergences(STOP) \;=\; \{\}$$

$$failures(STOP) \;=\; \{\langle\rangle\} \times \mathbf{P}\Sigma$$

$$divergences(SKIP) \;=\; \{\}$$

$$failures(SKIP) \;=\; (\{\langle\rangle\} \times \mathbf{P}(\Sigma-\checkmark))$$

$$\cup\,(\{\langle\checkmark\rangle\} \times \mathbf{P}\Sigma)$$

$$divergences(x \to P) \;=\; \{\langle x\rangle^\frown s | s \in\; divergences\,(P)\}$$

$$failures(x \to P) \;=\; \{(\langle\rangle, X) | X \subseteq \Sigma-\{x\}\}$$

$$\cup\,\{(\langle x\rangle^\frown s, X) | (s, X) \in\; failures\,(P)\}$$

$$divergences(P \; ; \; Q) \;=\; divergences(P)$$

$$\cup\; \left\{ \begin{array}{c} s^\frown t | s^\frown\langle\checkmark\rangle \in traces(P) \wedge s\checkmark\!-\!free \\ \wedge t \in divergences(Q) \end{array} \right\}$$

$$failures(P; Q) \;=\; \{(s, X) | s\checkmark\!-\!free \,\wedge\, (s, X \cup \langle\checkmark\rangle) \in\; failures\,(P)\}$$

$$\cup\; \left\{ \begin{array}{c} (s^\frown t, X) | s^\frown\langle\checkmark\rangle \in traces(P) \wedge s\checkmark\!-\!free \,\wedge \\ (t, X) \in failures(Q) \end{array} \right\}$$

$$\cup\,\{(s, X) | s \in\; divergences\,(P; Q)\}$$

$$\begin{array}{rl} divergences \\ (P \;[\![A|B]\!]\; Q) \end{array} = \left\{ \begin{array}{c} s^\frown t | s \in (A \cup B \cup \{\checkmark\})^* \wedge \\ \left(\begin{array}{c} \left(\begin{array}{c} s \upharpoonright (A \cup \{\checkmark\}) \in divergences(P) \wedge \\ s \upharpoonright (B \cup \{\checkmark\}) \in traces(Q) \end{array} \right) \\ \vee \left(\begin{array}{c} s \upharpoonright (B \cup \{\checkmark\}) \in divergences(Q) \wedge \\ s \upharpoonright (A \cup \{\checkmark\}) \in traces(P) \end{array} \right) \end{array} \right) \end{array} \right\}$$

$$failures(P \;[\![A|B]\!]\; Q) \;=\; \left\{ \begin{array}{c} (s, X \cup Y \cup Z) | s \in (A \cup B \cup \{\checkmark\})^* \\ \wedge X \subseteq (A \cup \{\checkmark\}) \wedge Y \subseteq (B \cup \{\checkmark\}) \wedge \\ Z \subseteq (\Sigma - (A \cup B \cup \{\checkmark\})) \\ \wedge (s \upharpoonright (A \cup \{\checkmark\}), X) \in\; failures\,(P) \\ \wedge (s \upharpoonright (B \cup \{\checkmark\}), Y) \in\; failures\,(Q) \end{array} \right\}$$

$$\cup\,\{(s, X) | s \in\; divergences\,(P[\![A|B]\!]Q)\}$$

Figure 1.4 – Denotational Semantics for CSP II

$$divergences(P \mid\mid\mid Q) = \left\{ \begin{array}{c} \exists s, t. \quad u \in merge(s, t) \wedge \\ \left(\begin{array}{c} (s \in divergences(P) \wedge t \in traces(Q)) \vee \\ (s \in traces(P) \wedge t \in divergences(Q)) \end{array} \right) \end{array} \right\}$$

$$failures(P \mid\mid\mid Q) = \left\{ \begin{array}{c} (u, X) \mid \exists s, t. \\ \left(\begin{array}{c} \left(\begin{array}{c} (s, X-\{\checkmark\}) \in failures(P) \wedge \\ (t, X) \in failures(Q) \end{array} \right) \vee \\ \left(\begin{array}{c} (s, X) \in failures(P) \wedge \\ (t, X-\{\checkmark\}) \in failures(Q) \end{array} \right) \end{array} \right) \wedge \\ u \in merge(s, t) \end{array} \right\}$$

$$\cup \ \{(s, X) \mid s \in divergences(P \mid\mid\mid Q)\}$$

$$divergences(P \sqcap Q) = divergences(P) \cup divergences(Q)$$

$$failures(P \sqcap Q) = failures(P) \cup failures(Q)$$

$$divergences(P \ \Box \ Q) = divergences(P) \cup divergences(Q)$$

$$failures(P \ \Box \ Q) = \left\{ \begin{array}{c} (s, X) \mid (s, X) \in failures(P) \cap failures(Q) \vee \\ \left(\begin{array}{c} s \neq \langle \rangle \wedge \\ (s, X) \in failures(P) \cup failures(Q) \end{array} \right) \end{array} \right\}$$

$$\cup \ \{(s, X) \mid s \in divergences(P \ \Box \ Q)\}$$

$$divergences(P \setminus x) = \left\{ \begin{array}{c} (s \upharpoonright (\Sigma - \{x\}))\,\hat{}\,t \mid \\ \left(\begin{array}{c} s \in divergences(P) \\ \vee (\forall n. s\,\hat{}\,\langle x \rangle^n \in traces(P)) \end{array} \right) \end{array} \right\}$$

$$failures(P \setminus x) = \{(s \upharpoonright (\Sigma - \{x\}), X) \mid (s, X \cup \{x\}) \in failures(P)\}$$

$$\cup \ \{(s, X) \mid s \in divergences(P \setminus \{x\})\}$$

$$divergences(f(P)) = \{f(s)t \mid s \in divergences(P)\}$$

$$failures(f(P)) = \{(f(s), X) \mid (s, f^{-1}(X)) \in failures(P)\}$$

$$\cup \ \{(s, X) \mid s \in divergences(f(P))\}$$

1.3 OPERATIONAL SEMANTICS

So far, we have encountered two ways of looking at communicating processes: first, as algebraic expressions, and second, in terms of abstract mathematical sets based on their observable behaviour. There is no obvious way of seeing from either of these representations how our processes might be realised on a machine. We need a more concrete approach – an operational model. The operational semantics of CSP is a mapping from CSP expressions to *state transition systems*. A state transition system is a labelled digraph where each vertex represents a *state* in which the process may rest. The outgoing arcs from each vertex represent the events that the process is ready to perform when in the associated state. The destination vertex of each of these arcs represents the new state that the process attains by performing the associated event. There is one particular vertex that is marked as the initial state of the process. A special event τ is used to represent concealed events or internal decisions. States that have outgoing τ-labelled arcs are called *unstable*. Those that do not are called *stable*.

Transition systems for certain processes that we have previously encountered are shown in Figure 1.5. Note that recursion is represented here by the presence of circuits in the digraphs.

Figure 1.5 – State Transition Systems

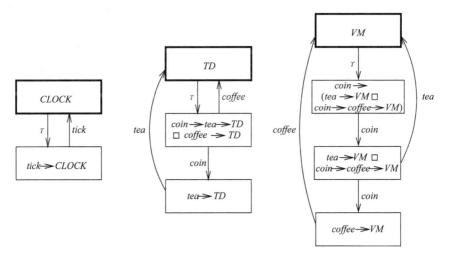

The operational semantics of CSP is defined by a set of inference rules that define a mapping from closed CSP terms to transition systems. Each clause consists of a (possibly empty) set of assertions $\{A_1, ..., A_n\}$ and a conclusion C presented in the form

$$\frac{A_1, ..., A_n}{C}$$

Consider, for example, the rules that define sequential composition.

$$\frac{P \xrightarrow{a} P'}{(P\,;\,Q) \xrightarrow{a} (P'\,;\,Q)}\,a \neq \checkmark$$

$$\frac{P \xrightarrow{\checkmark} P'}{(P\,;\,Q) \xrightarrow{\tau} Q}$$

The first clause states that if a process P can perform a certain event a, where a can be any event except for $\checkmark$, and its subsequent behaviour is then described by the process P', then process $P\,;\,Q$ can also perform a and its subsequent behaviour is described by $P'\,;\,Q$. The second clause tells us that if P can terminate straight away, by performing event $\checkmark$, then $P\,;\,Q$ can perform an internal event τ and then behave like Q.

The full set of operational rules for the subset of the CSP language that we are using is given in Figures 1.6 and 1.7. These clauses are taken from [Roscoe 1988a] and [Formal Systems 1993]. They may be used to systematically construct transition digraphs from systems of CSP equations, as is done by the refinement checking program FDR [Formal Systems 1993]. As an example, let us consider how the transition digraph for process TD, Figure 1.5, is constructed. First of all, the defining CSP equation is converted into a syntax tree as follows:

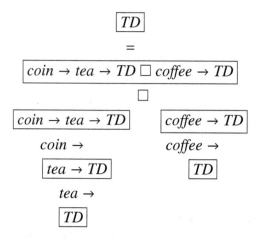

The syntax tree shows how the defining CSP term for TD is composed of operators acting on sub-processes. Each framed process term represents a potential state of TD or a state of one of its sub-processes. We can expand some of these straight away using the operational rule for event prefixing.

$$\boxed{coin \ \rightarrow \ tea \ \rightarrow \ TD} \ \xrightarrow{coin} \ \boxed{tea \ \rightarrow \ TD}$$

$$\boxed{tea \ \rightarrow \ TD} \ \xrightarrow{tea} \ \boxed{TD}$$

$$\boxed{coffee \ \rightarrow \ TD} \ \xrightarrow{coffee} \ \boxed{TD}$$

We are now ready to expand the external choice construct which gives us

$$\boxed{coin \ \rightarrow \ tea \ \rightarrow \ TD \ \Box \ coffee \ \rightarrow \ TD} \ \xrightarrow{coin} \ \boxed{tea \ \rightarrow \ TD}$$

$$\boxed{coin \ \rightarrow \ tea \ \rightarrow \ TD \ \Box \ coffee \ \rightarrow \ TD} \ \xrightarrow{coffee} \ \boxed{TD}$$

The rule for recursion enables us to make the following connection:

$$\boxed{TD} \ \xrightarrow{\tau} \ \boxed{coin \ \rightarrow \ tea \ \rightarrow \ TD \ \Box \ coffee \ \rightarrow \ TD}$$

It may not be immediately obvious how this follows from the rule for recursion, which is phrased in terms of the μ operator. The reason that it does follow is that we are actually using TD as an abbreviation for

$$\mu X . coin \ \rightarrow \ tea \ \rightarrow X \ \Box \ coffee \ \rightarrow X$$

It is now the case that every state reachable from TD has been expanded, and together they constitute a state-transition system for TD, which is

$$\left\{ \begin{array}{c} \boxed{TD} \ \xrightarrow{\tau} \ \boxed{coin \ \rightarrow \ tea \ \rightarrow \ TD \ \Box \ coffee \ \rightarrow \ TD} \\ \boxed{coin \ \rightarrow \ tea \ \rightarrow \ TD \ \Box \ coffee \ \rightarrow \ TD} \ \xrightarrow{coin} \ \boxed{tea \ \rightarrow \ TD} \\ \boxed{coin \ \rightarrow \ tea \ \rightarrow \ TD \ \Box \ coffee \ \rightarrow \ TD} \ \xrightarrow{coffee} \ \boxed{TD} \\ \boxed{tea \ \rightarrow \ TD} \ \xrightarrow{tea} \ \boxed{TD} \end{array} \right\}$$

(Note that states $coin \rightarrow tea \rightarrow TD$ and $coffee \rightarrow TD$ are not reachable from TD.) This gives us the finite-state machine shown in Figure 1.5. It is important to note that not all CSP expressions have finite operational representations. Some simple examples of infinite state processes are given in [Roscoe 1994].

It is straightforward to derive the failures and divergences of a process from its state transition system. However, there may be many operational representations of a single process, just as there may be many algebraic representations. It is shown in [Roscoe 1988a] that the denotational semantics of CSP, *i.e.*, the *Failures-Divergences* model, and the operational semantics are *congruent*. This means that if Φ is the mapping from operational semantics to failures and divergences, and **op** is the representation of a CSP operation in the operational model, and *op* is the representation of the same CSP operation in the denotational model, then for any process P in the operational model, we have

$$\Phi(\mathbf{op}(P)) = op(\Phi(P))$$

This means that the behaviour of a process predicted by its failures and divergences will be the same as that which can be observed in its operational representation. So, we may use the operational semantics of CSP in order to prove properties of process behaviour that are phrased in the *Failures-Divergences* model. This feature turns out to be particularly useful when the operational representation of a process is finite, although its failures and divergences are infinite, as is usually the case in practice. (More on this in Chapter 3.)

Figure 1.6 – Operational Semantics for CSP I

Primitive processes:

$$\overline{SKIP \xrightarrow{\checkmark} STOP}$$

Prefix:

$$\overline{(a \rightarrow P) \xrightarrow{a} P}$$

External choice:

$$\frac{P \xrightarrow{a} P'}{(P \,\square\, Q) \xrightarrow{a} P'} a \neq \tau$$

$$\frac{Q \xrightarrow{a} Q'}{(P\square Q) \xrightarrow{a} Q'} a \neq \tau$$

$$\frac{P \xrightarrow{\tau} P'}{(P \,\square\, Q) \xrightarrow{\tau} (P' \,\square\, Q)}$$

$$\frac{Q \xrightarrow{\tau} Q'}{(P \,\square\, Q) \xrightarrow{\tau} (P \,\square\, Q')}$$

Internal choice:

$$\overline{(P \sqcap Q) \xrightarrow{\tau} P}$$

$$\overline{(P \sqcap Q) \xrightarrow{\tau} Q}$$

Sequential composition:

$$\frac{P \xrightarrow{a} P'}{(P\,;\,Q) \xrightarrow{a} (P'\,;\,Q)}\,a \neq \checkmark$$

$$\frac{P \xrightarrow{\checkmark} P'}{(P\,;\,Q) \xrightarrow{\tau} Q}$$

Figure 1.7 – Operational Semantics for CSP II

Parallel composition:

$$\frac{P \xrightarrow{a} P'}{P\,|[\,A\,|\,B\,]|\,Q \xrightarrow{a} P'\,|[\,A\,|\,B\,]|\,Q}\,a \in (A - B - \{\checkmark\}) \cup \{\tau\}$$

$$\frac{Q \xrightarrow{a} Q'}{P\,|[\,A\,|\,B\,]|\,Q \xrightarrow{a} P\,|[\,A\,|\,B\,]|\,Q'}\,a \in (B - A - \{\checkmark\}) \cup \{\tau\}$$

$$\frac{P \xrightarrow{a} P'\ \ Q \xrightarrow{a} Q'}{P\,|[\,A\,|\,B\,]|\,Q \xrightarrow{a} P'\,|[\,A\,|\,B\,]|\,Q'}\,a \in (A \cap B) \cup \{\checkmark\}$$

Interleaving:

$$\frac{P \xrightarrow{a} P'}{P \,|||\, Q \xrightarrow{a} P' \,|||\, Q}\,a \neq \checkmark$$

$$\frac{Q \xrightarrow{a} Q'}{P \,|||\, Q \xrightarrow{a} P \,|||\, Q'}\,a \neq \checkmark$$

$$\frac{P \xrightarrow{\checkmark} P'\ \ Q \xrightarrow{\checkmark} Q'}{P \,|||\, Q \xrightarrow{\checkmark} P' \,|||\, Q'}$$

Hiding:

$$\frac{P \xrightarrow{a} P'}{(P\backslash A) \xrightarrow{\tau} (P'\backslash A)}\,a \in A \cup \{\tau\}$$

$$\frac{P \xrightarrow{a} P'}{(P\backslash A) \xrightarrow{a} (P'\backslash A)}\,a \notin A \cup \{\tau\}$$

Alphabet transformation:

$$\frac{P \xrightarrow{a} P'}{f(P) \xrightarrow{f(a)} f(P')}$$

Recursion:

$$\frac{}{\mu X \bullet F(X) \xrightarrow{\tau} F(\mu X \bullet F(X))}$$

1.4 LANGUAGE EXTENSIONS

The core CSP syntax described above is very abstract and lacks certain useful features found in conventional sequential and parallel programming languages. The extensions outlined below are useful for writing more detailed specifications.

Sometimes, we define processes with parameters, such as

$$BUFF(in, out) = in \rightarrow out \rightarrow BUFF(in, out)$$

This is a process schema, rather than an actual process. It defines a CSP process for each combination of parameter values. CSP parameters may be integers, real numbers, events, sets, matrices, *etc.*

A *communication* is a special type of event described by a pair $c.v$, where c is the name of the channel on which the event takes place and v is the value of the message that is passed.

The set of messages communicable on channel c is defined

$$type(c) = \{v \mid c.v \in \Sigma\}$$

Input and output are defined as follows. A process that first outputs v on channel c and then behaves like P is defined

$$(c!v \rightarrow P) = (c.v \rightarrow P)$$

Outputs may involve expressions of parameters, such as $P(x) = c!x^2 \rightarrow Q$. The expressions are evaluated according to the appropriate laws.

A process that is initially prepared to input any value x communicable on the channel c and then behave like $P(x)$ is defined.

$$(c?x \rightarrow P(x)) = \square_{v:type(c)}(c.v \rightarrow P(v))$$

It is usual for a communication channel to be used by at most two processes at any time: one for input and the other for output. However, this restriction is not enforced in the modern version of CSP.

Another important aspect to real programming languages is the use of conditionals. Let b be a Boolean expression (either true or false). Then

$$P \triangleleft b \triangleright Q \qquad (\text{``}P \text{ if } b \text{ else } Q\text{''})$$

is a process that behaves like P if the value of expression b is true, or like Q otherwise.

These extensions are useful for specifying fine detail during the later stages of program refinement. At the design stage, we shall tend to stick to abstract, non-deterministic definitions of processes. The deadlock issue will be addressed at this point. In this way, we shall build robust program for which deadlock freedom cannot be compromised by implementation decisions made at a later stage.

1.5 DEADLOCK ANALYSIS

Terminology and Fundamental Results
The problem of the 'deadly embrace' was first reported by E.W. Dijkstra relating to resource sharing [Dijkstra 1965]. It has proved a popular topic of research ever since. Most of the early work was presented in an informal manner, for instance, [Chandy and Misra 1979], largely due to the lack of a suitable mathematical model for concurrency at the time. But, in 1985–1986, S.D. Brookes, A.W. Roscoe, and N. Dathi presented some powerful techniques for reasoning about deadlock based upon the solid mathematical foundations of CSP. A major benefit of their approach is that it relies only on local analysis of pairs of processes and simple topological properties of the network configuration. This makes it suitable for analysing networks of arbitrary size. The terminology introduced here is taken from the following sources: [Brookes and Roscoe 1985b], [Roscoe and Dathi 1986], and [Brookes and Roscoe 1991].

We consider a *network, V*, which is a list of processes $\langle P_1, ..., P_n \rangle$. Associated with each process P_i is an alphabet αP_i. The corresponding process, $\|_{i=1}^n (P_i, \alpha P_i)$, is denoted as $PAR(V)$.

We view a network as consisting of a static collection of everlasting components. Parallel programs do not need to terminate to produce useful results, and deadlock analysis is simplified if we can cast termination aside. Henceforth, we shall only consider processes that are non-terminating, *i.e.*, they never perform the event $\checkmark$ (although they may still be constructed from sub-processes that do terminate).

A process P can deadlock after trace s if and only if $(s, \Sigma) \in failures(P)$. We say P is *deadlock-free* if

$$\forall s : traces(P). \quad (s, \Sigma) \notin failures(P)$$

Note that this definition of deadlock freedom also excludes any process that can diverge (by axiom 7 of the *failures* model), which seems reasonable as divergence is every bit as undesirable a phenomenon as deadlock. Network V is said to be deadlock-free if the process $PAR(V)$ is deadlock-free.

The following lemma describes how individual sequential processes may be constructed free of deadlock. Used in conjunction with the algebraic laws of CSP, it also enables us to prove deadlock freedom for certain small networks of processes by manipulation into a sequential form. Unfortunately, this technique does not scale at all well to large networks because the resulting CSP terms usually increase in length in a manner exponentially proportional to the number of processes that constitute the network.

Lemma 1 (Roscoe-Dathi 1986) *Suppose the definition of the process P uses only the following syntax*

$$Process ::= SKIP \mid$$
$$event \rightarrow Process \mid$$
$$Process \; ; \; Process \mid$$
$$Process \sqcap Process \mid$$
$$Process \;\square\; Process \mid$$
$$f(Process) \mid$$
$$name \mid$$
$$\mu \, name \bullet Process$$

where 'name' denotes a process variable, but P contains no free process variables, is divergence-free, and every occurrence of SKIP in P is directly or indirectly followed by a ';' to prevent successful termination. Then P is deadlock-free $\square$

If every component process P_i of a network is deadlock-free, we say that the network is *busy*. A network is *triple-disjoint* if no event requires the participation of more than two processes. We shall restrict our attention to networks that are both busy and triple disjoint. This will enable us to analyse networks for deadlock freedom purely by the local analysis of neighbouring pairs of processes.

We observe the convention that communication channels are used in only one direction and between only two processes. We call this the I/O convention. This guarantees that whenever two processes are ready to communicate on a particular channel, the communication can go ahead. Sometimes, when we are not concerned about the data that are communicated, it is convenient to substitute a channel name for communication events in a process description. For instance, we might write $a \rightarrow SKIP$ instead of $a?x \rightarrow SKIP$. This is known as *abstraction*. If we can prove freedom from deadlock for an abstracted version of a network, then the property will also hold for the original. A formal treatment of this is given in [Roscoe 1995].

A *network state* of V is defined as a trace s of $PAR(V)$, together with a sequence $\langle X_1, ..., X_n \rangle$ of refusal sets X_i, such that for each i,

$$(s \upharpoonright \alpha P_i, X_i) \in failures(P_i)$$

We say that a network state is *maximal* if each of its refusal sets is maximal, *i.e.*, if $(s, \langle X_1, ..., X_n \rangle)$ is a maximal state of V then for each process P_i, there is no failure $(s \upharpoonright \alpha P_i, Y)$ such that $X_i \subset Y$.

When we consider deadlock properties, we find that all the relevant information is carried by the maximal network states, as the more events that an individual process refuses, the more likely deadlock becomes. So, from now on, all network states will be taken to be maximal, as this simplifies the analysis.

There is a close relationship between a network state and the operational states of the processes within. Suppose we visualise a network as a collection of state transition systems, one representing each process. A network state is then rather like a cross-section of the network. The trace s tells us what each process has done so far, and each refusal set X_i corresponds to a particular stable state of process P_i, telling us exactly what it is refusing to do on the next step. For instance, the network,

$$\langle VM, TD \rangle$$

for which the transition systems are illustrated in Figure 1.5, has a network state,

$$(\langle coin \rangle, \langle \{coffee\}, \{coin, coffee\} \rangle)$$

which corresponds to the situation where the tea drinker has inserted a coin into the vending machine. The vending machine is then in operational state $tea \rightarrow VM \; \square \; coin \rightarrow coffee \rightarrow VM$, refusing event $coffee$ and prepared to accept $\{coin, tea\}$. The tea drinker is in operational state $tea \rightarrow TD$, refusing $\{coin, coffee\}$ and prepared only to accept tea.

The following lemma characterises network states where deadlock is present.

Lemma 2 (Roscoe-Dathi 1986) *PAR(V) can deadlock after trace s if and only if there is a network state* $(s, \langle X_1, ..., X_n \rangle)$ *such that*

$$\bigcup_{i=1}^{n} (X_i \cap \alpha P_i) = \bigcup_{i=1}^{n} \alpha P_i$$

☐

This follows easily from the definitions. Such a state is called a *deadlock state*.

Suppose that, in a particular state $\sigma = (s, \langle X_1, ..., X_n \rangle)$, there is a process P_i, which is ready to communicate with P_j, i.e.,

$$(\alpha P_i - X_i) \cap \alpha P_j \neq \{\}$$

We say that P_i is making a *request* to P_j in state σ, which is written as

$$P_i \overset{\sigma}{\rightarrow} P_j$$

29

We say that this request is *ungranted* if P_j also refuses to respond to P_i's request, *i.e.*,

$$\alpha P_i \cap \alpha P_j \subseteq X_i \cup X_j$$

This is written as

$$P_i \overset{\sigma}{\to} \bullet P_j$$

The set of shared events within a network is known as its *vocabulary*, written as Λ.

$$\Lambda = \bigcup_{i \neq j} (\alpha P_i \cap \alpha P_j)$$

Sometimes, we are only interested in ungranted requests from P_i to P_j when neither process is able to communicate outside the vocabulary of the network, *i.e.*, in addition to the above

$$(\alpha P_i - X_i) \cup (\alpha P_j - X_j) \subseteq \Lambda$$

Then, we say that P_i is making an ungranted request to P_j *with respect to* Λ. We write

$$P_i \overset{\sigma,\Lambda}{\to} \bullet P_j$$

We say that P_i is *blocked* in network state σ of V if

$$\exists j. \ \ P_i \overset{\sigma}{\to} P_j \ \ \text{and} \ \ P_i \overset{\sigma}{\to} P_k \implies P_i \overset{\sigma,\Lambda}{\to} \bullet P_k$$

which means that P_i is ready to engage in a communication with at least one other process, but no process that P_i wishes to communicate with is able to do so. Neither P_i nor any process that it wishes to communicate with is able to perform any event outside the vocabulary of V.

The following lemma is derived from the above definitions:

Lemma 3 (Roscoe-Dathi 1986) *If σ is a state of a triple disjoint, busy network V, then σ is a deadlock state if, and only if, every process in V is blocked in state σ* $\square$

This result may be interpreted graphically. We define the *wait-for digraph* of a network state as follows. It is a digraph that has a vertex for every process P_i and arcs from any blocked process to each process for which it is waiting. Figure 1.8 shows examples of wait-for digraphs, which illustrate Lemma 3.

Figure 1.8 – Wait-for Digraphs

No deadlock (P_4 and P_5 can run)

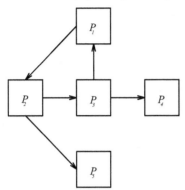

Deadlock (all processes blocked)

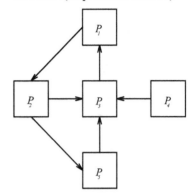

We may deduce an interesting feature of deadlock states. Consider a deadlock state of a busy, triple-disjoint network V. By Lemma 3, there is at least one ungranted request from every process, with respect to the vocabulary of V. So, starting with any process P_{i_1}, we may build an arbitrarily long sequence of ungranted requests as follows:

$$P_{i_1} \overset{\sigma,\Lambda}{\to} \bullet P_{i_2} \overset{\sigma,\Lambda}{\to} \bullet P_{i_3} \cdots$$

As there are only a finite number of processes, P_i, this sequence must eventually arrive back at a process that it has already visited, *i.e.*, there is a *cycle of ungranted requests*

$$P_{i_m} \overset{\sigma,\Lambda}{\to} \bullet P_{i_{m+1}} \overset{\sigma,\Lambda}{\to} \bullet \dots \overset{\sigma,\Lambda}{\to} \bullet P_{i_{m+k}} \overset{\sigma,\Lambda}{\to} \bullet P_{i_m}$$

Hence, we have proved the following result.

Theorem 1 *In any deadlock state of a triple disjoint, busy network, there is a cycle of ungranted requests with respect to its vocabulary* □

Roscoe and Dathi made use of this fact to establish a method for investigating the deadlock properties of networks that involves only local checking. The crucial idea behind this technique is as follows. If a function is defined on the states of processes in a network that is strictly decreasing along any chain of ungranted requests, then there can never be a cycle of ungranted requests and hence no deadlock. An example of using this technique will be given in the next chapter.

Theorem 2 (Roscoe-Dathi 1986) *Let $V = \langle P_1, ..., P_n \rangle$ be a busy, triple-disjoint network with vocabulary Λ. If there exist functions f_i, from the* *failures of each process P_i to a strict partial order $(S, >)$, such that whenever $\sigma = \left(s, \langle X_i, X_j \rangle\right)$ is a state of the subnetwork $\langle P_i, P_j \rangle$*

$$P_i \overset{\sigma, \Lambda}{\to} \bullet P_j \implies f_i \left((s \upharpoonright \alpha P_i, X_i)\right) > f_j \left((s \upharpoonright \alpha P_j, X_j)\right)$$

then V is deadlock-free. Or if there exist similar functions g_i, such that

$$P_i \overset{\sigma, \Lambda}{\to} \bullet P_j \implies g_i \left((s \upharpoonright \alpha P_i, X_i)\right) \geq g_j \left((s \upharpoonright \alpha P_j, X_j)\right)$$

then any deadlock state $\delta = (s, \langle X_1, ..., X_n \rangle)$ of V contains a cycle of ungranted requests,

$$P_{i_1} \overset{\delta, \Lambda}{\to} \bullet P_{i_2} \overset{\delta, \Lambda}{\to} \bullet ... P_{i_m} \overset{\delta, \Lambda}{\to} \bullet P_{i_1}$$

such that

$$g_{i_1} \left((s \upharpoonright \alpha P_{i_1}, X_{i_1})\right) = g_{i_2} \left((s \upharpoonright \alpha P_{i_2}, X_{i_2})\right) = ... = g_{i_m} \left((s \upharpoonright \alpha P_{i_m}, X_{i_m})\right) \square$$

The existence of a cycle of ungranted requests does not always mean deadlock has occurred. The cycle might subsequently be broken by the intervention of a process from outside the cycle.

Deadlock-free networks exist that sometimes develop cycles of ungranted requests, and this theorem is not sufficiently powerful to prove them so. Dathi's thesis contains a hierarchy of stronger techniques, together with a classification of different levels of deadlock freedom that they may be used to establish [Dathi 1990].

By treating cycles of length two as a special case, we can arrive at a useful extension to Theorem 1. We say that two processes P_i and P_j are in *conflict* with respect to Λ in network state σ if each one is trying to communicate with the other but cannot agree on which event to perform, *i.e.,*

$$P_i \overset{\sigma, \Lambda}{\longrightarrow} \bullet P_j \wedge P_j \overset{\sigma, \Lambda}{\longrightarrow} \bullet P_i$$

A conflict is basically a cycle of ungranted requests of length two. It is said to be *strong* if one of the processes is able to communicate *only* with the other process, *i.e.,*

$$\left((\alpha P_i - X_i) \subseteq \alpha P_j\right) \vee \left((\alpha P_j - X_j) \subseteq \alpha P_i\right)$$

We call a network where strong conflict can never occur *strong conflict-free.*

Theorem 3 (Brookes-Roscoe 1991) *In any deadlock state of a triple disjoint, busy, strong conflict-free network, there is a cycle of ungranted requests with respect to its vocabulary of length greater than two.*

Proof. Consider the wait-for digraph of a deadlock state σ of such a network. Starting at any node P_{i_j}, we can form a sequence of arbitrary length

$$P_{i_1} \xrightarrow{\sigma,\Lambda} \bullet P_{i_2} \xrightarrow{\sigma,\Lambda} \bullet P_{i_3} \ldots$$

with the property that $P_{i_j}, P_{i_{j+1}}$, and $P_{i_{j+2}}$ are all distinct for each j. For if $P_{i_{j+1}}$ has an ungranted request back to P_{i_j}, the two processes are in conflict and as this cannot be a strong conflict, $P_{i_{j+1}}$ must also have an ungranted request to some other process, which may then be selected as $P_{i_{j+2}}$. This sequence will eventually cross itself, which means that there must be a cycle of ungranted requests of length greater than two□.

The property of strong conflict-freedom may be established by pairwise analysis of processes in the network, and in this way, it may be checked for networks of arbitrary size.

Brookes and Roscoe used this result to develop another technique for proving deadlock freedom by showing that a cycle of ungranted requests cannot occur. This relies on the processes in the network obeying a rather special condition, which is somewhat in the nature of a *design rule*.

Theorem 4 (Brookes-Roscoe 1991) *Let $V = \langle P_1, ..., P_N \rangle$ be a busy, triple-disjoint, strong-conflict-free network, such that whenever a process P has an ungranted request to another process Q, then Q has previously communicated with P and has done so more recently than with any other process. It follows that V is deadlock-free.*

Proof. Consider a deadlock state σ of a strong-conflict-free network V. By Theorem 3, there must exist a cycle of ungranted requests, of length at least three, as follows:

$$P_{i_1} \xrightarrow{\sigma,\Lambda} \bullet P_{i_2} \xrightarrow{\sigma,\Lambda} \bullet \ldots P_{i_k} \xrightarrow{\sigma,\Lambda} \bullet P_{i_1}$$

Now, suppose that the most recent communication between two consecutive elements of this cycle was between P_{i_h} and $P_{i_{h+1}}$ (where addition is modulo k – the length of the cycle). Consider that the ungranted request from $P_{i_{h-1}}$ to P_{i_h}. P_{i_h} has communicated with $P_{i_{h+1}}$ more recently than it has with $P_{i_{h-1}}$. This means that any strong-conflict-free network that deadlocks does not satisfy the conditions of the theorem. It follows that a network that obeys the conditions of the theorem is deadlock-free□.

This result has been used by Roscoe to develop a complex and sophisticated message routing algorithm [Roscoe 1988b]. A generalisation of the theorem is given in [Roscoe 1995].

Livelock
In high-level concurrent programming languages, such as occam, it is conventional for communication channels between two processes to be concealed from the environment. This can potentially cause a form of divergence known as *livelock*. We say that a network is *livelock-free* if it can never perform an infinite sequence of internal or hidden actions, *i.e.,*

$$divergences(PAR(V)\backslash\Lambda) = \{\}$$

Roscoe discovered a useful technique (detailed in [Dathi 1990]) for establishing this important property. It is described here in a slightly simplified form.

Theorem 5 (Roscoe 1982) *Suppose* $V = \langle P_1, ..., P_N \rangle$ *is a triple-disjoint network of non-divergent processes such that for every* P_i *in V*

$$P_i \backslash \left(\cup_{j<i} \left(\alpha P_i \cap \alpha P_j \right) \right) \quad \text{is divergence-free}$$

then $PAR(V)\backslash\Lambda$ *is divergence-free*□

In other words, if no process in a network can ever perform an infinite sequence of communications with its predecessors, then the network is livelock-free. (This can be proved by induction.) This theorem is found to be useful in many cases, although it requires careful ordering of the processes within the network to be effective.

Network Decomposition
The communication architecture of a triple-disjoint network may be represented by a *communication graph*. This consists of a vertex to represent each process and an edge to connect each pair of processes with overlapping alphabets. The next theorem describes how deadlock analysis of a network may be broken down into the analysis of a collection of smaller components by the removal of disconnecting edges (see Appendix B) from the communication graph.

Theorem 6 (Brookes-Roscoe 1991) *Consider the communication graph of a network V with a set of disconnecting edges which separates the network into components*

$$\langle V_1, ..., V_k \rangle$$

If each pair of processes joined by a disconnecting edge is conflict-free with respect to Λ and each subnetwork V_j is deadlock-free, then so is $V\square$.

A proof of this theorem is given in [Brookes and Roscoe 1991].

This result is useful for the hierarchical construction of networks. It offers a safe way of connecting subsystems together without introducing any risk of deadlock.

Hiding

An important feature of reasoning with CSP is the use of the concealment operator, which enables us to hide those events that we are not interested in. This can greatly simplify the deadlock analysis of a network.

Lemma 4 *If $P\backslash C$ is deadlock-free, then P is deadlock-free$\square$*

Used with CSP law 1.30, this result enables us to add extra external communications to the component processes of a deadlock-free network. Deadlock freedom will be preserved as long as the behaviour of each component is unchanged when these events are concealed.

Lemma 5 *Suppose V is a network $\langle P_1, ..., P_n \rangle$. Let V' be a network $\langle P_1', ..., P_n' \rangle$, such that*

$$P_i' \backslash \left(\alpha P_i' - \alpha P_i \right) = P_i$$
$$i \neq j \implies \left(\alpha P_i' - \alpha P_i \right) \cap \alpha P_j' = \{\}$$

then

$$PAR(V) = PAR(V') \backslash \bigcup_{i=1}^{n} (\alpha P_i' - \alpha P_i)$$

Furthermore, if V is deadlock-free, then so is V'.

Proof.

$$PAR(V) = \|_{i=1}^{n}(P_i, \alpha P_i)$$
$$= \|_{i=1}^{n}(P_i' \setminus (\alpha P_i' - \alpha P_i), \alpha P_i)$$
$$= (\|_{i=1}^{n}(P_i', \alpha P_i')) \setminus \bigcup_{i=1}^{n}(\alpha P_i' - \alpha P_i) \quad \text{by application of law 1.30}$$
$$= PAR(V') \setminus \bigcup_{i=1}^{n}(\alpha P_i' - \alpha P_i)$$

It now follows from Lemma 4 that V' inherits deadlock freedom from V □

Refinement

CSP processes are related by a complete partial order $\sqsubseteq$, which we described in Section 1.2. $Q \sqsubseteq P$ means that every behaviour pattern that is possible for P is also possible for Q. We say that Q is a *specification* for P and that P is a *refinement* of Q.

The operation of parallel composition with any particular process is known to be *monotonic*, *i.e.*, order-preserving, with respect to this partial ordering (in fact, all CSP operations are). This leads us to the following observation:

Lemma 6 *Suppose that* $V = \langle P_1, ..., P_N \rangle$ *and* $V' = \langle P_1', ..., P_N' \rangle$ *are networks where*

$$\forall i : \{1, ..., N\}. \quad P_i \sqsubseteq P_i'$$

then $PAR(V) \sqsubseteq PAR(V')$ □

In particular, this means that if V is deadlock-free, then so is V'. Similarly, if V is livelock-free, then so is V'.

This result makes an important statement about the way in which we should design and build concurrent systems, which has already been hinted at. At the design stage, we should specify each of our components in as abstract a manner as possible. Important properties of the system as a whole that are shown to hold at this stage, such as freedom from deadlock and divergence, will be preserved as we gradually refine each component into the finished product.

2

DESIGN RULES FOR DEADLOCK FREEDOM

INTRODUCTION

The problem of determining whether any given concurrent system can ever deadlock is similar to the famous halting problem of Turing machines – it is undecidable. This means that there can never be an algorithmic method for proving deadlock freedom that will work in the general case [Mairson 1989].

If the system consists only of finite-state processes, then we can always theoretically check deadlock freedom by exhaustive state analysis, but as the number of states of the system as a whole tends to be exponentially proportional to the number of processes, this technique is only viable for very small networks.

The previous chapter details efficient proof techniques that will work in a wide variety of cases, but there is no guarantee that the existing systems will be amenable to them in practice. What is needed is a set of rules that enable us to guarantee deadlock freedom at the design stage before the major work of building the system has been done.

Here, we describe three practical design paradigms that may be used for this purpose.

- Networks of *cyclic-ordered* processes: Each process behaves according to a fixed cyclic communication pattern. It is useful for computationally intensive tasks, such as finite-element analysis or neural network simulation.

- Client-server systems: Processes communicate according to a master-slave protocol. Applications include process farms and message routing systems.
- User-resource systems: User processes compete for shared resources. Applicable to distributed databases and operating systems.

These rules have the joint advantages of being easy to use and also being backed up with mathematical rigour. We use the theoretical results of the previous chapter to prove them correct and to show how they may be combined hierarchically. When used in this way, they are suitable for the construction of a rich variety of concurrent systems.

2.1 CYCLIC PROCESSES

Many parallel applications consist of large arrays of simple processes with fixed cyclic communication patterns. P.H. Welch discovered some deadlock-prevention rules for certain processes of this type [Welch 1987]. He presented these results informally in the context of the occam programming language. We shall now state and prove them in the formal context of CSP.

A process P is called *I/O-SEQ* if it operates cyclically such that, once per cycle, it communicates on a finite set of input channels I in parallel, then it communicates on a finite set of output channels O also in parallel.

Abstracting away any data that is passed, we can write an *I/O-SEQ* process, with input channel set I, and output channel set O with the following CSP equation:

$$I/O\text{-}SEQ(I, O) = (\||_{c:I}\ c \rightarrow SKIP); (\||_{d:O}\ d \rightarrow SKIP); I/O\text{-}SEQ(I, O)$$

$$\alpha I/O\text{-}SEQ(I, O) = I \cup O$$

A process that communicates on all its channels in parallel on every cycle is called *I/O-PAR*. In CSP, we write it like this

$$I/O\text{-}PAR(I, O) = (\||_{c:I \cup O}\ c \rightarrow SKIP); I/O\text{-}PAR(I, O)$$

$$\alpha I/O\text{-}PAR(I, O) = I \cup O$$

When *I/O-PAR* and *I/O-SEQ* processes are combined in a network, we observe the *I/O* convention. Recall that this means that a channel may be used by at most two processes – one for input and the other for output. *The connection digraph* of a network of *I/O-PAR* and *I/O-SEQ* processes is constructed in the following way. A vertex is used to represent each process, and an arc is used to represent each shared channel, directed from the process for which it is an output channel towards the process for which it is an input channel. A sequence of channels that forms a path in the connection diagram of a network is called a *data-flow path*; a sequence of channels that forms a circuit is called a *data-flow circuit*.

These processes may be composed in ways that guarantee deadlock freedom according to some simple design rules.

Rule 1 (Welch 1987) *Any network of I/O-PAR processes is deadlock-free.*

In other words, any network constructed exclusively from *I/O-PAR* components, no matter how large, will never deadlock.

Rule 2 (Welch 1987) *A connected network of I/O-SEQ processes is deadlock-free if, and only if, it has no data-flow circuits.*

Rule 3 (Welch 1987) *A connected network of I/O-SEQ and I/O-PAR processes is free of deadlock if, and only if, it has no data-flow circuits which pass through only I/O-SEQ processes.*

We shall now prove the correctness of these rules using Theorem 2 (page 31). Note that Rules 1 and 2 are corollaries of Rule 3, so it is only necessary to prove the last result.

Proof. Let $V = \langle P_1, \dots, P_n \rangle$ be a connected network of *I/O-SEQ* and *I/O-PAR* processes. Then for each maximal failure (s, X) of P_i, we define a variant function, $f_i((s, X))$, which calculates the number of complete cycles of *I/O* operations that P_i has completed after trace s. This is given by

$$f_i((s, X)) = \left\lfloor \frac{|s|}{|\alpha P_i|} \right\rfloor$$

From the definitions, we can deduce that a process in this network can never be waiting for an *I/O-SEQ* process that has performed more cycles than it has and can only be waiting to communicate with an *I/O-PAR* process that has performed less cycles than it has. So, let σ be a state $(s, \langle X_i, X_j \rangle)$ of the sub-network $\langle P_i, P_j \rangle$. Then, if P_j is *I/O-SEQ*

$$P_i \xrightarrow{\sigma, \Lambda} \bullet P_j \Longrightarrow f_i((s \restriction \alpha P_i, X_i)) \geq f_j((s \restriction \alpha P_j, X_j))$$

but if P_j is *I/O-PAR*

$$P_i \xrightarrow{\sigma, \Lambda} \bullet P_j \Longrightarrow f_i((s \restriction \alpha P_i, X_i)) > f_j((s \restriction \alpha P_j, X_j))$$

Suppose that *V* has a deadlock state σ, then by Theorem 2, there must be a cycle of ungranted requests in state σ such that the variant function of each process is the same. It follows from the above observations that all the processes in the cycle of ungranted requests must be *I/O-SEQ*. Each of these processes must be waiting for input from its successor in the cycle, so the cycle of ungranted requests corresponds to a data-flow circuit (in the opposite direction) passing through only *I/O-SEQ* processes.

Otherwise, suppose that the network contains a data-flow circuit through *I/O-SEQ* processes. Each process on this circuit is bound to come to a halt during its first cycle to wait forever for input from its predecessor. No process in the network can ever advance more than one cycle beyond any of its neighbours in the connection digraph, so deadlock will eventually ensue because the network is connected□

Figure 2.1 illustrates examples of networks constructed from *I/O-SEQ* and *I/O-PAR* elements. One of these has a data-flow circuit passing exclusively through *I/O-SEQ* processes and so deadlocks; the other has no such circuit and so is deadlock-free.

Composite Processes

Sometimes, we may build a component from *I/O-SEQ* and *I/O-PAR* processes and then wish to replicate it many times in a larger system. The next rule describes how, in the right circumstances, we may treat such a component as a single process for the purpose of deadlock analysis. We will start with some new definitions.

Figure 2.1: Networks of *I/O-SEQ* and *I/O-PAR* Processes

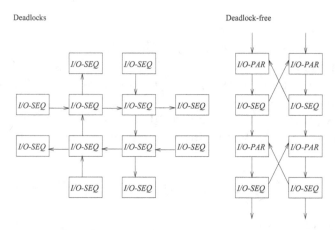

If a connected network, *V*, of *I/O-SEQ* processes has no data-flow circuits, we say that *PAR(V)* is a *composite-I/O-SEQ* process.

The input and output channels of *PAR(V)* are taken to be those channels that do not belong to the vocabulary of *V* and so are used by only a single process. We call these the *external* channels of *V*.

If a connected network, *V*, of *I/O-SEQ* and *I/O-PAR* components has neither a dataflow circuit passing through only *I/O-SEQ* processes nor a data-flow path from an *I/O-SEQ* process with an external input channel to an *I/O-SEQ* process with an external output channel passing through only *I/O-SEQ* processes, we say that *PAR(V)* is a *composite-I/O-PAR* process.

We find that Welch's rules generalise to composite processes as follows:

Rule 4 (Welch 1987) *A connected network V of composite-I/O-SEQ and composite-I/O-PAR processes is deadlock-free if, and only if, it has no data-flow circuits which pass through only composite-I/O-SEQ processes.*

Proof. Let *V'* be the network of *I/O-PAR* and *I/O-SEQ* processes that may be derived from *V* by breaking each process down into its basic components. This rule follows from Rule 3 by proving that *V* contains a data-flow circuit through *composite-I/O-SEQ* processes if, and only if, *V'* contains a data-flow circuit through *I/O-SEQ* processes.

In graph-theoretic terms, the connection diagram of *V* is a *contraction* of that of *V'* (see Appendix B). Suppose that *V* contains a data-flow circuit through only *composite-I/O-SEQ* processes, then, clearly, *V'* contains a data-flow circuit passing only through *I/O-SEQ* processes.

Alternatively, suppose that a data-flow circuit, *C*, is contained within *V'*, passing only through *I/O-SEQ* processes. Under the contraction of connection diagrams from *V'* to *V*, *C* maps either to a directed *closed trail* of *V* or to a single vertex. (Note that a closed trail differs from a circuit in that its vertices are not necessarily distinct –it may 'cross' itself.) The latter option may be eliminated immediately as it implies the presence of a data-flow circuit within a composite process, which is prohibited by definition. The former option implies that *V* contains a directed closed trail through *composite-I/O-SEQ* processes, because there can be no path through a *composite-I/O-PAR* process that does not cross a simple *I/O-PAR* element. Any directed, closed trail of *V* entails at least one circuit.

So *V* contains a data-flow circuit through *composite-I/O-SEQ* processes if and only if *V'* contains a data-flow circuit through *I/O-SEQ* processes, and the required result may now be deduced from Rule 3□

It is useful to note that basic *I/O-SEQ* and *I/O-PAR* processes are also *composite-I/O-SEQ* and *composite-I/O-PAR*, respectively. This enables us to build a deadlock-free network from a mixture of basic and composite processes.

Example – Emulating VLSI Circuits

Welch originally formulated these design rules in order to emulate VLSI circuits using the occam programming language. He used Rule 4 to construct various 'circuits' hierarchically. For example, a 'latch' component is shown in Figure 2.2. This is built from two *I/O-PAR* 'nand' gates and two *I/O-SEQ* 'delta' processes (which simply duplicate their input signal). The latch component is *composite-I/O-PAR*.

Welch used this technique to predict the behaviour of complex electronic circuits prior to their realisation in silicon. He was able to construct deadlock-free networks with hundreds of thousands of processes using design Rules 1 to 4. These rules have subsequently been used for many other applications by occam programmers (*e.g.*, see [Macfarlane 1992]). Rules 1 and 2 were also reported by [Roscoe and Dathi 1986].

A General Rule

Dijkstra and Scholten developed a rule for cyclic processes that communicate exactly once with each of their neighbours on each cycle in a fixed sequence [Dijkstra 1982]. This was extended by Roscoe and Dathi to allow sets of communications to be performed in parallel, as with Welch's rules. Here, we generalise all these results to produce a partial order-based rule.

A *cyclic-PO* process is a process P with a finite set of communication channels C, which operates cyclically, communicating on each of its channels once per cycle. The order of communication is governed by a *strict partial order* $(C, >)$, whereby P becomes ready to communicate on a channel c for the nth time, once it has completed its $(n-1)$th cycle, and has communicated on all the channels below c by $>$ on its nth cycle. This can be defined formally as follows:

$$CYCLIC\text{-}PO(C, >) = C2(C, \{\}, >)$$
$$C2(C, DONE, >) = C2(C, \{\}, >)$$
$$\triangleleft DONE = C \triangleright$$
$$\square_{x:mins(C-DONE,>)} \, x \rightarrow C2(C, DONE \cup \{x\}, >)$$

$$\alpha CYCLIC\text{-}PO(C, >) = C$$

Figure 2.2: *LATCH:* **A Composite-*I/O-PAR* Process**

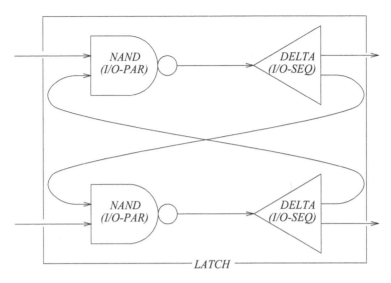

where $mins(Y, >)$ is defined as the minimal elements of subset Y of C, given by

$$mins(Y, >) = \{y \in Y | \nexists z \in Y.\ y > z\}$$

Now, we consider a network of cyclic-PO processes, $V = \langle P_1 \ldots P_N \rangle$, where

$$P_i = CYCLIC\text{-}PO(\alpha P_i, >_i)$$

The set of communication channels of the network as a whole, $\bigcup_{i=1}^{N} \alpha P_i$, is called αV. We use symbol $\triangleright$ to represent the aggregate of the various partial orderings, $>_i$, i.e.,

$$c_i \triangleright c_j \iff \exists k.\quad c_i >_k c_j$$

The direction of data-flow circuit along communication channels, if any, is irrelevant to the deadlock properties of cyclic-PO networks. Sometimes, it is meaningless to assign any direction to a channel. For this reason, we shall here consider the *connection graph* of a network rather than the connection digraph. This is constructed in the same way, except that it is undirected.

An *undirected, closed trail of dependent channels* is a sequence of channels of αV, $\langle c_1 \ldots c_m \rangle$, which forms a closed trail in the connection graph of V (see Appendix B for definitions), and satisfies

$$c_1 \triangleright c_2 \triangleright \ldots \triangleright c_m \triangleright c_1$$

Theorem 7 *A connected network of cyclic-PO processes is deadlock-free if, and only if, it has no undirected, closed trail of dependent channels.*

Proof. Suppose there exists an undirected, closed trail of dependent channels, such that

$$c_1 \triangleright c_2 \triangleright \ldots \triangleright c_m \triangleright c_1$$

No communication can ever take place on any of these channels, so the processes they are connected to will never complete their first *I/O* cycle. No cyclic-PO process can ever have advanced more than one *I/O* cycle beyond its neighbours in the connection graph of V, so there is a limit to the number of events that any component process can execute. Hence, deadlock will eventually ensue.

Now suppose instead that we have arrived at a deadlock state σ of V. Every process is unable to proceed and has at least one ungranted request (with respect to Λ).

Consider any ungranted request $P_{i_1} \xrightarrow{\sigma,\Lambda} \bullet P_{i_2}$, where P_{i_1} wants to communicate on some channel c_1 for the n_1th time, but P_{i_2} is refusing to participate. Either P_{i_2} and P_{i_1} have both completed the same number of *I/O* cycles, but P_{i_2} has not yet communicated on all its channels below c_1 by $\triangleright$ on the current cycle, or P_{i_2} has completed one less *I/O* cycle than P_{i_1}. It follows that P_{i_2} is waiting to communicate on some channel c_2 for the n_2th time, where either $(n_1 = n_2) \wedge (c_1 \triangleright c_2)$ or $n_1 > n_2$.

We can repeat this argument to construct an arbitrarily long sequence of pairs

$$(c_1, n_1), (c_2, n_2), (c_3, n_3) \ldots$$

Where $\quad \forall i. \quad ((n_i = n_{i+1}) \wedge (c_i \triangleright c_{i+1})) \vee (n_i > n_{i+1})$

The channels of this sequence correspond to a walk in the underlying graph of V.

The decreasing sequence $n_1, n_2, n_3 \ldots$ must have a limit, *i.e.*,

$$\exists p. \quad \forall j \geq p. \quad n_j = n_p$$
$$\text{Hence, } c_p \triangleright c_{p+1} \triangleright c_{p+2} \triangleright \ldots$$

As αV is finite, this sequence must eventually repeat a term, *i.e.*,

$$\exists q, r. \quad c_{p+q} \triangleright c_{p+q+1} \triangleright \ldots \triangleright c_{p+q+r} = c_{p+q}$$
$$\text{where } c_{p+q}, \ldots, c_{p+q+r-1} \text{ are all distinct.}$$

This sequence is represented by a closed trail in the connection graph of $V\square$

This theorem describes the deadlock properties of networks of cyclic processes in general. If each process can complete its first I/O cycle, the network will never deadlock.

It is worth mentioning a special case of cyclic-PO processes. We define a *cyclic-LOP process* to be a cyclic-PO process where $(\alpha P, >)$ takes the form of a *linearly ordered partition*. This means that αP is partitioned into subsets $\lambda_1, \dots, \lambda_m$ such that

$$\forall c_1 : \lambda_1. \quad \forall c_2 : \lambda_2. \quad \dots \quad \forall c_m : \lambda_m. \quad c_1 > c_2 > \dots > c_m$$
$$\forall i : \{1, \dots, m\}. \quad \forall c, c' : \lambda_i \quad \neg c > c'$$

The *I/O-PAR* and *I/O-SEQ* cyclic processes, defined by Welch, both have *cyclic-LOP* communication patterns. The $>$ relation is empty for an *I/O-PAR* process. For an *I/O-SEQ* process, $c_i > c_j$ if and only if c_i is an output channel and c_j is an input channel. For a network, V, of cyclic-LOP processes, we can derive a result with a simpler topological requirement than for cyclic-PO processes. This is a slight extension of a theorem due to Roscoe and Dathi.

An *undirected, circuit of dependent channels* is a sequence of channels of $\alpha V, \langle c_1 \dots c_m \rangle$, which forms a circuit in the connection graph of V, and satisfies

$$c_1 \triangleright c_2 \triangleright \dots \triangleright c_m \triangleright c_1$$

Theorem 8 *A connected network consisting of cyclic-LOP processes is free of deadlock if, and only if, it has no undirected circuit of dependent channels.*

This is proved in virtually the same manner as Welch's rules. In a deadlock state of a network of cyclic-LOP processes, there must be a cycle of ungranted requests where each process has performed the same number of I/O cycles. The crucial observation is that if P_i has an ungranted request to P_j, trying to perform some event c and both processes have performed the same number of I/O cycles, then *every* event that P_j is ready to perform is beneath c in the partial ordering $>_j\square$

The result that Roscoe and Dathi proved was the same as this, except that it enforced the extra restriction that at most one channel be permitted between any two processes.

These theorems may be too complicated to be considered design rules in their own right; however, a suite of design rules for computationally intensive parallel systems can be derived. For instance, Welch's rules drop out as simple corollaries. Here is an example of a new design rule.

Rule 5 *A connected network of cyclic-PO processes is deadlock-free if, and only if, there exists a labelling of the connection graph, given by* $l : \alpha V \rightarrow N$, *which satisfies*

$$c_i \triangleright c_j \implies l(c_i) > l(c_j)$$

Proof. We use the technique of *reductio ad absurdum.* Suppose the conditions of the rule hold, and yet V can deadlock. Then, by Theorem 7, there is a sequence of channels satisfying

$$c_1 \triangleright c_2 \triangleright ... \triangleright c_m \triangleright c_1$$
$$\implies l(c_1) > l(c_2) > ... l(c_m) > l(c_1)$$
$$\implies l(c_1) > l(c_1) \quad \#$$

Conversely, if V is deadlock-free, by the nature of its construction, it must have a trace s of finite length, which includes every element of αV. We label each element of αV according to the position of its first appearance in s to derive a labelling that satisfies the conditions of the theorem. This completes the proof□

To design a network using this rule, we first draw a connection graph (or digraph if we prefer) and label each channel with a numeric value, representing a logical order. Then, if each process is implemented as a cyclic-PO process capable of communicating on its channels in order of increasing value, the network is deadlock-free. (When a process has more than one channel of the same value, it should be implemented to communicate in parallel on those channels.)

Example – A Toroidal Cellular Automaton
To demonstrate this approach, we consider a *4 × 4* cellular automaton program where each cell compares its state with those of its four neighbours in strict, clockwise order. This is based on a program described in [Dewdney 1989]. The idea is that each cell maintains an integer state, and whenever it finds that its state is exactly one less than that of a neighbour, it changes state to match. (All comparisons are done using modulo arithmetic.) When a large grid is used, some interesting patterns evolve.

Blind to the risk of deadlock, we might give each cell process an identical communication pattern, such as defined by the following processes, where each cell communicates with its neighbours in the order left, up, right, then down.

$$CELL(i,j) = LEFT(i,j)$$
$$LEFT(i,j) = (e.i.j.left \rightarrow SKIP \mid\mid\mid e.(i-1).j.right \rightarrow SKIP); \; UP(i,j)$$
$$UP(i,j) = (e.i.j.up \rightarrow SKIP \mid\mid\mid e.i.(j-1).down \rightarrow SKIP); \; RIGHT(i,j)$$
$$RIGHT(i,j) = (e.i.j.right \rightarrow SKIP \mid\mid\mid e.(i+1).j.left \rightarrow SKIP); \; DOWN(i,j)$$
$$DOWN(i,j) = (e.i.j.down \rightarrow SKIP \mid\mid\mid e.i.(j+1).up \rightarrow SKIP); \; LEFT(i,j)$$

$$\alpha CELL(i,j) = \left\{ \begin{array}{llll} e.i.j.left, & e.i-1.j.right, & e.i.j.up, & e.i.j-1.down \\ e.i.j.right, & e.i+1.j.left, & e.i.j.down, & e.i.j+1.up \end{array} \right\}$$

In this process definition, all integer arithmetic is *modulo 4*. The network is given by

$$\langle CELL(0,0),...,CELL(0,3),...,CELL(3,0),...,CELL(3,3)\rangle$$

This arrangement leads to immediate deadlock because there exist many undirected, closed trails of dependent channels. We tackle this problem by labelling each channel of the network and then recoding each process to communicate on its channels according to the ascending order of its labels. The labelling scheme shown in Figure 2.3 allows each component to communicate in strict clockwise order as required. But cells alternate as to whether to start by communicating on the left or on the right. This gives us a new definition for *CELL* as follows:

$$CELL(i,j) = LEFT(i,j) \lhd ((i+j) \; modulo \; 2 = 0) \rhd RIGHT(i,j)$$

An implementation of this network, programmed in occam2, is given in [Martin *et al* 1994].

In practice, it would be desirable to add extra channels to this network to monitor the state of each cell and reset the system when required. Use of the cyclic-PO paradigm would require that each channel be used on every *I/O* cycle, which might be unnecessary. In the next section, Theorem 7 will be extended to allow processes to communicate on a subset of their channels on any given *I/O* cycle (as long as neighbouring processes are in agreement as to which channels are to be used) and also to allow the channel ordering to be changed between successive cycles.

Multi-phase Communication Patterns

A *multi-phase-PO* process is a deadlock-free process, *P*, with a set of communication channels, αP, which operates cyclically, communicating once on a predefined subset of its channels on each cycle. On its *k*th cycle, *P* communicates according to a partial order

$$(\alpha^{(k)}P, >^{(k)})$$

where $\alpha^{(k)}P \subseteq \alpha P$: P communicates on channel c on its kth cycle if and only if $c \in \alpha^{(k)}P$, in which case it becomes ready to do so once it has completed its $(k-1)$th cycle and has communicated on all the channels of $\alpha^{(k)}P$ below c by $>^{(k)}$ on its kth cycle□

We say that a network of *multi-phase-PO* processes, $V = \langle P_1 \dots P_N \rangle$, is *concordant* if neighbouring processes agree on which subset of channels to use on each *I/O* cycle:

$$\forall k : N - \{0\}. \ \forall i,j : \{0,1,\dots N\}. \quad \alpha^{(k)}P_i \cap \alpha P_j = \alpha P_i \cap \alpha^{(k)}P_j$$

Figure 2.3: Connection Digraph with Channel Labelling

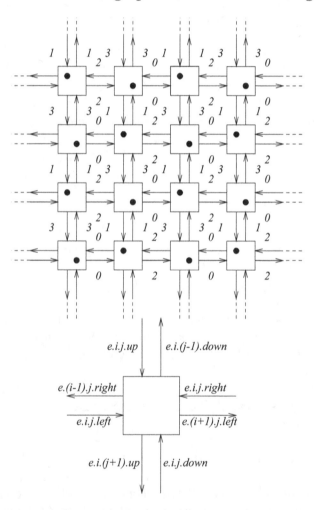

Theorem 9 *A connected, concordant network of multi-phase-PO processes is free of deadlock if, and only if, $\forall k : N - \{0\}$ there is no undirected, closed trail of $\triangleright^{(k)}$ dependent channels*□

The proof of this is virtually identical to that of Theorem 7, and we can derive a similar design rule.

Rule 6 *If there exists a partial labelling of the channels of a network of multi-phase-PO processes, for every I/O cycle, given by the partial functions $l_k : \alpha V \mapsto N$, which satisfies*

$$c_i \triangleright^{(k)} c_j \Rightarrow l_k(c_i) > l_k(c_j)$$
$$\forall i : \{1, \ldots, N\}. \quad \alpha P_i \cap domain(l_k) = \alpha^{(k)} P_i$$

then the network is deadlock-free□

Figure 2.4 illustrates how this rule may be used to add a control process to the toroidal cellular automaton. In this design, each cell communicates bidirectionally with the control process after the completion of every fourth cycle of communication with its neighbours.

2.2 CLIENT-SERVER PROTOCOL

The cyclic paradigm may be used effectively to solve many common problems in parallel computing. However, for certain problems, it is too restrictive in the respect that it enforces a pre-determined communication pattern. In practice, we often need to allow the communication patterns of processes to vary according to external requirements. A more flexible design rule from this perspective is the *Client-Server Protocol*. This was originally formulated by P. Brinch Hansen in the context of operating systems [Brinch Hansen 1973]. It has since been adapted by Welch, G.R.R. Justo, and C.J. Willcock as a means of designing deadlock-free concurrent systems using occam [Welch *et al* 1993]. The version of the protocol presented here is a formal adaptation and extension of the ideas of these authors, which were stated informally.

The main requirement is that processes communicate on each one of their channels, either as a *client* or as a *server*, according to a strict protocol. A network of client-server processes is deadlock-free if it has no cycle of client-server relationships.

A *basic client-server* CSP process P has a finite set of external channels partitioned into separate *bundles*, each of which has a type in relation to P, which is either *client* or *server*. Each channel bundle consists of *either* a pair of channels, a *requisition* and an *acknowledgement*, $\langle r, a \rangle$, *or* a single channel (which we call a *drip*) $\langle d \rangle$. (This allows client-server conversations to be either one-way or two-way.) We write the set of client bundles of P as *clients*(P) and the server bundles as *servers*(P).

Figure 2.4: Multi-phase Channel Labelling

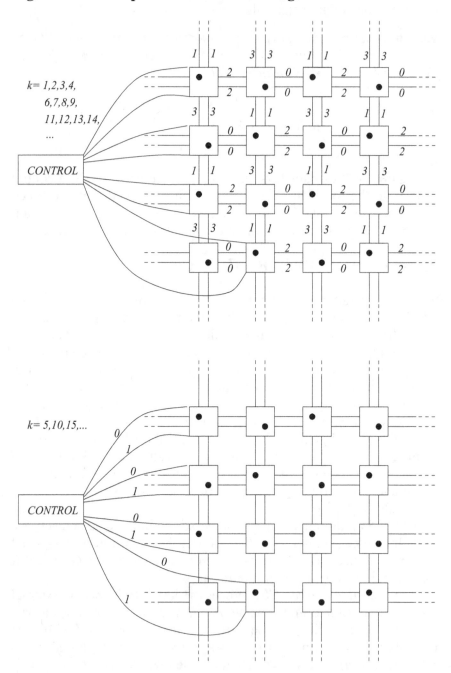

In the subsequent analysis, the event of communication on a channel is again represented purely by the channel name, ignoring any data that is passed. The purpose of this is clarity and simplicity. Following this convention, a basic client-server process, P, must obey the following rules:

(a) P is divergence-free, deadlock-free, and non-terminating.

$$\forall (s, X) : failures\ (P).\quad X \neq \Sigma$$

(b) When P is in a stable state (no internal activity possible), *either* it is ready to communicate on all its *requisition* and *drip* server channels *or* it is ready to communicate on none of them. In CSP terms, this means that *maximal* refusal sets of P include either all the requisition and drip server channels or none of them, *i.e.*,

$$\forall (s, X) : failures(P).\quad X\quad maximal \implies$$

$$\left(\begin{array}{l} (\forall \langle d \rangle : servers(P).\quad d \notin X) \wedge \\ (\forall \langle r, a \rangle : servers(P).\quad r \notin X) \end{array}\right) \vee$$

$$\left(\begin{array}{l} (\forall \langle d \rangle : servers(P).\quad d \in X) \wedge \\ (\forall \langle r, a \rangle : servers(P).\quad r \in X) \end{array}\right)$$

(c) P always communicates on any bundle pair $\langle r, a \rangle$, in the sequence $r, a, r, a, ...$, *i.e.*,

$$\forall \langle r, a \rangle: clients(P) \cup servers(P).\quad \forall s : traces(P).$$
$$1 \geq (s \downarrow r - s \downarrow a) \geq 0$$

(d) When P communicates on a client *requisition* channel, it must guarantee to accept the corresponding *acknowledgement, i.e.*,

$$\forall \langle r, a \rangle : clients(P).\quad \forall (s, X) : failures(P).$$
$$s \downarrow r > s \downarrow a \implies (a \notin X)$$

When we construct a *client-server* network V from a set of client-server processes $\langle P_1, ..., P_N \rangle$, each client bundle of a process must *either* be a server bundle of exactly one other process *or* consist of channels external to the network. Similarly, each server bundle of any process must either be a client bundle of exactly one other process or be external to the network. No other communication between processes is permitted, *i.e.*,

$$\forall i \in \{1, \dots, N\}. \quad \forall s \in clients(P_i)$$
$$Either \quad \exists! j. \quad j \neq i \wedge s \in servers(P_j)$$
$$Or \ let \quad s = \langle s_1, \dots, s_k \rangle \quad then \quad \{s_1, \dots, s_k\} \cap \Lambda = \{\}$$

$$\forall i \in \{1, \dots, N\}. \quad \forall s \in servers(P_i)$$
$$Either \quad \exists! j. \quad j \neq i \wedge s \in clients(P_j)$$
$$Or \ let \quad s = \langle s_1, \dots, s_k \rangle \quad then \quad \{s_1, \dots, s_k\} \cap \Lambda = \{\}$$

$$i \neq j \implies \quad Let \quad (clients \ P_i \cap servers \ P_j) \cup (clients \ P_j \cap servers \ P_i) =$$
$$\{\langle s_{1,1}, \dots, s_{1,k_1} \rangle, \dots, \langle s_{m,1}, \dots, s_{m,k_m} \rangle\}$$
$$Then \quad \alpha P_i \cap \alpha P_j = \{s_{1,1}, \dots, s_{1,k_1}, \dots, s_{m,1}, \dots, s_{m,k_m}\}$$

The *client-server digraph* of a client-server network consists of a vertex representing every process and an arc representing each shared bundle, directed from the process for which it is of type client towards that for which it is of type server.

Rule 7 (Client-Server Theorem) *A client-server network, composed of basic processes, which has a circuit-free client-server digraph, is deadlock-free.*

Proof. First, we observe that the matching requirements for client and server bundles within a network enforce triple-disjointedness within a client-server network. Rule **(a)** ensures that basic client-server networks are also busy.

Let V be a client-server network, composed of basic processes, the client-server digraph of which contains no circuit. Suppose it has a deadlock state σ. There must be a cycle of ungranted requests in state σ by Theorem 1 (page 31). As the client-server digraph is circuit-free, this cycle of ungranted requests cannot consist entirely of requests from client to server or vice versa. It must contain a subsequence

$$P_i \xrightarrow{\sigma, \Lambda} \bullet P_j \xrightarrow{\sigma, \Lambda} \bullet P_k$$

where P_i communicates with P_j as client to server and P_j communicates with P_k as server to client. (Note that if the cycle of ungranted requests has a length of only two, then P_i and P_k are the same process.)

We shall now show that the basic client-server protocol renders this situation impossible. First, we note that by rules **(c)** and **(d)**, P_j can only be waiting to communicate with P_k on a server requisition or drip channel; an acknowledgement is never refused. Hence, P_j is ready to communicate on all its server requisition and drip channels by rule **(b)**. So, P_i must be waiting for an acknowledgement from P_j. However, by rule **(c)**, P_j must have already acknowledged every previous requisition event in order to be ready to communicate on all its requisition channels. So, P_i cannot have an ungranted request to P_j after all. This contradiction proves that the system has no deadlock state□

Example – A Simple Process Farm

We consider an application where computing-intensive tasks are performed in parallel using a standard farm network configuration. A farmer employs n foremen, each of whom is responsible for m workers. When a worker process becomes idle, it reports the result of any work done to its foreman using channel $a.i.j$, where j denotes worker and i denotes foreman. The foreman reports this on channel $c.i$ to the farmer, who, in turn, replies with a new task using channel $d.i$. The foreman then assigns the new task to the worker with channel $b.i.j$. Here, the relationship between worker and foreman and the relationship between foreman and farmer are both client to server.

The CSP communication patterns of the component processes are given as follows:

$$FARMER = \Box_{i=0}^{n-1} c.i \rightarrow d.i \rightarrow FARMER$$
$$clients(FARMER) = \{\}$$
$$servers(FARMER) = \{\langle c.0, d.0\rangle, \dots, \langle c.(n-1), d.(n-1)\rangle\}$$
$$\alpha FARMER = \{\langle c.0, \dots, c.(n-1), d.0, \dots, d.(n-1)\rangle\}$$

$$FOREMAN(i) = \Box_{j=0}^{m-1} a.i.j \rightarrow c.i \rightarrow d.i \rightarrow b.i.j \rightarrow FOREMAN(i)$$

$$clients(FOREMAN(i)) = \{\langle c.i,d.i\rangle\}$$
$$servers(FOREMAN(i)) = \{\langle a.i.0, b.i.0\rangle, \dots, \langle a.i.(m-1), b.i.(m-1)\rangle\}$$
$$\alpha FOREMAN(i) = \{a.i.0, \dots, a.i.(m-1), b.i.0, \dots, b.i.(m-1), c.i,d.i\}$$

$$WORKER(i,j) = a.i.j \rightarrow b.i.j \rightarrow WORKER(i,j)$$

$$clients(WORKER(i,j)) = \{\langle a.i.j,b.i.j\rangle\}$$
$$servers(WORKER(i,j)) = \{\}$$
$$\alpha WORKER(i,j) = \{a.i.j,b.i.j\}$$

It is straightforward to verify that each process obeys the basic client-server protocol. The client-server digraph is illustrated in Figure 2.5. It has no circuits; hence, the network is guaranteed deadlock-free.

Polling on a Channel

The technique of *polling* on a channel is a means by which a process can attempt to communicate on a channel without the risk of becoming blocked. In high-level implementation languages, this is achieved by the use of time-outs, possibly of zero duration. The version of CSP that we are using is untimed, so there is no direct equivalent to this. However, polling may still be represented using the available syntax. Consider the process

$$(in \rightarrow P \,\square\, timeout \rightarrow Q) \backslash timeout$$

This process cannot become blocked trying to communicate on channel *in*, because it is always able to perform the internal event *timeout*.

Figure 2.5: Client-Server Digraph for FARM

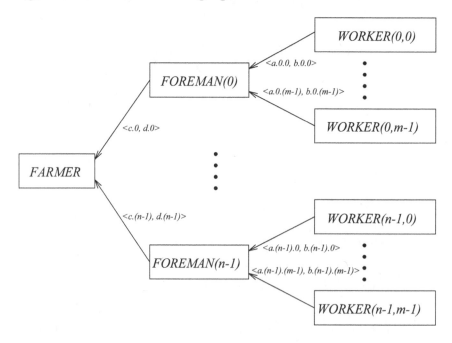

While a process is attempting to poll a channel, its state is unstable. Note that rule **(b)** of the basic client-server definition only applies to stable states. This means that the restriction that a process must either offer its services to all its clients or none of them at a given time may be overcome if polling is used. (However, one has to be very careful in order to avoid introducing divergence.) An example of using polling in a client-server network is given in [Martin and Welch 1996].

Composite Processes

A *composite* client-server process V is a client-server network $\langle P_1, \ldots, P_N \rangle$ composed solely from basic client-server processes, of which the client-server digraph contains no circuits; we define

$$clients(V) = \left(\bigcup_{i=1}^{N} clients(P_i) - \bigcup_{j=1}^{N} servers(P_j) \right)$$

$$servers(V) = \left(\bigcup_{i=1}^{N} servers(P_i) - \bigcup_{j=1}^{N} clients(P_j) \right)$$

In other words, the client and server bundles of V are those of the component processes P_i that are not paired off.

We represent a composite client-server process with a single vertex in a client-server digraph. The following result shows that this is consistent with the composition rule governing basic processes.

Rule 8 (Client-Server Closure) *A client-server network, composed of composite processes, with a circuit-free client-server digraph, is deadlock-free.*

Proof. Starting with a network such as described in the statement of the theorem with client-server digraph D, consider the client-server digraph D' of the network, which is derived when each composite process is separated back into its basic components. Digraph D is a contraction of D'. Suppose that D' contains a circuit. By definition, this cannot be local to a single composite process, and so it must map onto a closed trail in D. But as D has no circuit, it has no closed trail either – a contradiction. So, D' has no circuit, and the result follows from Rule 7□

It is important to note that any basic client-server process is itself a composite client-server (although the reverse is not true). Hence, we can apply the result to mixtures of composite and basic processes. This rule is clearly useful for designing networks hierarchically. Complex subnetworks may be reused with ease. Black-box processes that have been shown to abide by the composite client-server specifications may be safely incorporated.

However, the rule is too weak in some circumstances, as we shall demonstrate below. We need to find a generalisation.

We define a dependence relationship $\gg$ between server bundles and client bundles of a composite client-server process V as follows: if $x \in servers(V)$ and $y \in clients(V)$, then $x \gg y$ means that there is a path from the process with server bundle x to that with client bundle y, in the client-server digraph of V.

Figure 2.6: Composite Client-Server Process

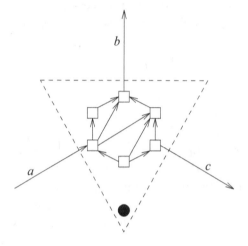

Figure 2.6 shows a hypothetical composite client-server process *BLACKBOX*, with external client-server channel bundles a, b, and c. Here, we have

$$servers(BLACKBOX) = \{a\}$$
$$clients(BLACKBOX) = \{b, c\}$$
$$a \gg b \ , \ \neg(a \gg c)$$

We construct an *exploded* client-server digraph of a network of composite processes in the following way: The digraph contains a vertex for every client and server bundle of each process. If v and v' are vertices representing bundles b and b' of the same composite process P_i, we draw an arc from v to v' if, and only if, $b \gg b'$ in P. If v and v' represent bundles of different processes P and P', then we draw an arc from v to v' if, and only if, both vertices represent the same channel bundle, v as a client bundle and v' as a server bundle.

We can derive the following result from these definitions.

Rule 9 *A client-server network, composed of composite client-server processes and with a circuit-free exploded client-server digraph, is deadlock-free.*

Proof. Starting with a network such as described in the statement of the theorem, consider the client-server digraph D' of the network, which is derived when each composite process is separated back into its basic components. Suppose that this contains a circuit. This must be of the form

$$\left\langle \begin{array}{l} a_1, b_{1,1}, b_{1,2}, \dots, b_{1,n_1}, a_2, b_{2,1}, b_{2,2}, \dots, \\ b_{2,n_2}, \dots, a_m, b_{m,1}, b_{m,2}, \dots, b_{m,n_m} \end{array} \right\rangle$$

where each subsequence $\langle b_{k,1}, \dots, b_{k,n_k} \rangle$ corresponds to a path through the client-server digraph of one of the original composite client-server processes, say P_k, and each arc a_k represents a channel bundle shared by two such composite processes P_{k-1} and P_k (where arithmetic is modulo m).

In the exploded client-server digraph of the original network, let each external channel bundle a of composite process P be represented by a vertex $a.P$. Then, each bundle a_k is represented by two *vertices*, say $a_k.P_{k-1}$ and $a_k.P_k$, because bundle a_k is shared by processes P_{k-1} and P_k. These two vertices will be joined by an arc. Now for each pair of bundles a_k, a_{k+1}, it is clear that $a_k \gg a_{k+1}$. Hence, each pair of vertices $a_k.P_k, a_{k+1}.P_k$ will also be joined by an arc. So, the exploded client-server digraph must contain a circuit

$$\langle (a_1.P_1, a_2.P_1), (a_2.P_1, a_2.P_2), \dots, (a_n.P_n, a_1.P_n), (a_1.P_n, a_1.P_1) \rangle$$

This is a contradiction, so there is no circuit in D', and the result is obtained by Rule 7□

Figure 2.7 displays two representations of a network constructed from six copies of *BLACKBOX* (with suitably relabelled channels): the client-server digraph and an exploded client-server digraph. The former contains a circuit, so we cannot use Rule 8 to show that the network is deadlock-free. However, the latter contains none. So, the network *is* deadlock-free by Rule 9.

Note that when 'exploding' a composite process, it is not always necessary to allocate a new vertex to every client or server bundle. Sometimes, we can use a single node to represent several client or server bundles without losing any information. This depends on the structure of the relation $\gg$.

Figure 2.7: Client-Server Digraph and Exploded Client-Server Digraph

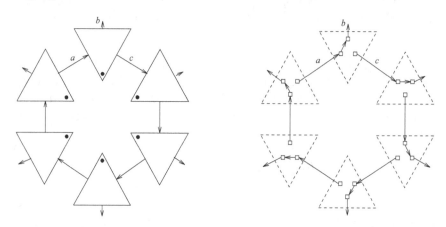

The benefit of Rules 8 and 9 is that we avoid repeating superfluous information in the diagrams we draw to design our programs. Instances of complex subnetworks are reduced to single nodes (or simplified representations when Rule 8 is too weak).

Adding a Client-Server Interface to an Arbitrary Network

Rules 8 and 9 make available a hierarchical approach to software construction based on multiple layers of the client-server model. It would also be nice to be able to use other paradigms to design subnetworks and then wrap them up with a client-server interface for inclusion in a wider context.

Here, we consider how to modify an arbitrary network so that it appears as a single basic client-server process in its environment.

We start with a deadlock-free network $V = \langle P_1, \dots, P_n \rangle$, where each process P_i is itself divergence-free, deadlock-free, and non-terminating. We want to add external communications to the components of this network to make it behave like a single basic client-server process. The resulting network will be called

$$V' = \langle P'_1, \dots, P'_n \rangle$$

where each process P'_i performs events in the alphabet of P_i and possibly additional events, which are external to the network, *i.e.*,

$$i \neq j \implies (\alpha P'_i - \alpha P_i) \cap \alpha P'_j = \{\}$$

The basic rule of thumb is that we may freely add client connections to any component process P_i, but we may add server connections to at most one such process.

Adherence to the following rules will guarantee that V' will behave as a single basic client-server process.

1. The additional channels of each process P'_i are partitioned into client and server bundles, and P'_i must obey the basic client-server protocol on these bundles.

   (The client-server bundles of V' are taken to be the union of those of each component, which will be disjoint. It is clear that V' will adhere to rules **(c)** and **(d)** of the basic client-server protocol if each process P'_i does.)

2. No more than one process P'_i may have *server* connections.

   (This is to ensure that V' obeys rule **(b)** of the basic protocol. This restriction may be avoided if polling is used.)

3. The new connections added to each process P_i must not interfere with its internal behaviour, *i.e.*,

$$P'_i \backslash (\alpha P'_i - \alpha P_i) = P_i$$

   (By Lemma 5, this condition guarantees that V' is deadlock-free, divergence-free, and non-terminating –rule **(a)** of the basic client-server protocol.)

Example – Adding a Flexible Control Mechanism

In Section 2.1, we designed a deadlock-free toroidal cellular array monitored by a control process to be constructed using the *multi-phase-PO* protocol. That approach required monitoring to be performed at fixed, predetermined intervals. A more flexible design is to add client connections to each cell, served by the control process. The new version looks like this.

$CELL'(i,j) = LEFT'(i,j) \lhd (i+j) \ modulo \ 2 = 0 \rhd RIGHT'(i,j)$

$CHAT(i,j) = SKIP \sqcap out.i.j \rightarrow in.i.j \rightarrow SKIP$

$LEFT'(i,j) = (e.i.j.left \rightarrow SKIP \ ||| \ e.(i-1).j.right \rightarrow SKIP);$
$\qquad\qquad CHAT(i,j); UP'(i,j)$

$UP'(i,j) = (e.i.j.up \rightarrow SKIP \ ||| \ e.i.(j-1).down \rightarrow SKIP);$
$\qquad\qquad CHAT(i,j); RIGHT'(i,j)$

$$RIGHT'(i,j) = (e.i.j.right \rightarrow SKIP \ ||| \ e.(i+1).j.left \rightarrow SKIP);$$
$$CHAT(i,j); DOWN'(i,j)$$
$$DOWN'(i,j) = (e.i.j.down \rightarrow SKIP \ ||| \ e.i.(j+1).up \rightarrow SKIP);$$
$$CHAT(i,j); LEFT'(i,j)$$

$$\alpha CELL'(i,j) = \left\{ \begin{array}{llll} e.i.j.left, & e.i-1.j.right, & e.i.j.up, & e.i.j-1.down \\ e.i.j.right, & e.i+1.j.left, & e.i.j.down, & e.i.j+1.up \\ & in.i.j, & out.i.j & \end{array} \right\}$$

After each interaction with a neighbour, the cell may non-deterministically decide to talk to a *CONTROL* process, implemented as follows:

$$CONTROL = \square_{i=0}^{3} \square_{j=0}^{3} \ out.i.j \rightarrow in.i.j \rightarrow CONTROL$$

We have added a client bundle of the form

$$\langle out.i,j, in.i.j \rangle$$

to each cell. No server bundles have been added, and the additional channels do not affect the internal working of each process, i.e.,

$$CELL'(i,j) \backslash \{in.i.j, \ out.i.j\} = CELL(i,j)$$

This may be proved using the algebraic laws of CSP. It follows that the complete cellular array now appears as a single basic client-server process in its environment. The client-server digraph that results is shown in Figure 2.8. This contains no circuits, so the entire system is deadlock-free. It is now a simple matter to build extra client-server components onto the system, such as a user interface and a graphics handler.

Figure 2.8: Adding Client-Server Connections

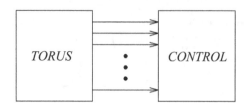

2.3   RESOURCE ALLOCATION PROTOCOL

The Resource Allocation Protocol was discussed briefly in the Introduction section. It will now be formalised, based on the treatment given in [Roscoe and Dathi 1986]. Then, an extended version will be presented that allows resources to be built on to the existing deadlock-free networks.

A *user-resource* network consists of a set of user processes $\{U_1, \ldots, U_N\}$ that compete for a linearly ordered set of resource processes $(\{R_1, \ldots, R_M\}, >)$, which have the following communication pattern:

$$R_j = \square_{i:\{1,\ldots,N\}} (claim_{ij} \rightarrow release_{ij} \rightarrow R_j)$$

Each resource j is initially ready to be claimed by any user process i using channel $claim_{ij}$. Then, once it has been claimed, it waits to be released on channel $release_{ij}$ before returning to its initial state. Note that in this abstract model, any details of message passing corresponding to the *claim* and *release* events are omitted.

Clearly, the channels $claim_{ij}$ and $release_{ij}$ are only meant to be used by user process U_i, i.e.,

$$k \neq i \implies \{claim_{ij}, release_{ij}\} \cap \alpha U_k = \{\}$$

We assume that each user process U_i is deadlock-free and non-terminating. It never tries to *claim* a resource that it already holds, nor to *release* one that it does not, i.e.,

$$\forall s : traces(U_i). \quad 1 \geq (s \downarrow claim_{ij} - s \downarrow release_{ij}) \geq 0$$

Rule 10 (Resource Allocation Protocol) *Consider a user-resource network V constructed from users $\{U_1, \ldots, U_N\}$ and resources $(\{R_1, \ldots, R_M\}, >)$. Suppose that no user process ever attempts to acquire a higher resource than any that it already holds, i.e.,*

$$\forall s : traces(U_i).$$
$$(s \downarrow claim_{ij} > s \downarrow release_{ij}) \wedge (R_k > R_j) \implies$$
$$s^\frown \langle claim_{ik} \rangle \notin traces(U_i)$$

and also that it never communicates with any other user process

$$i \neq j \implies \alpha U_i \cap \alpha U_j = \{\}$$

Then the network is deadlock-free.

Proof. Suppose the condition of the protocol is adhered to, yet there is a deadlock state σ. So, there exists a cycle of ungranted requests by Theorem 1 (page 31), which must be of the following form due to the bipartite nature of the network:

$$U_{i_1} \xrightarrow{\sigma} \bullet R_{j_1} \xrightarrow{\sigma} \bullet U_{i_2} \xrightarrow{\sigma} \bullet R_{j_2} \dots U_{i_k} \xrightarrow{\sigma} \bullet R_{j_k} \xrightarrow{\sigma} \bullet U_{i_1}$$

Here, user U_{i_1} wants to claim resource R_{j_1}, which is already held by user U_{i_2}, which wants to claim resource R_{j_2}, etc. This implies the following contradiction:

$$R_{j_1} > R_{j_2} > \dots > R_{j_k} > R_{j_1} \ \#$$

We conclude that the network can never deadlock$\square$

The Dining Philosophers network can be modelled in CSP as follows:

$$PHIL(i) = takes.i.i \to takes.i.(i-1) \to eats.i \to$$
$$drops.i.(i-1) \to drops.i.i \to PHIL(i)$$

$$\alpha PHIL(i) = \{takes.i.i, takes.i.(i-1), eats.i, drops.i.(i-1),$$
$$drops.i.i\}$$

$$FORK(j) = \square_{i=0}^{4} takes.i.j \to drops.i.j \to FORK(j)$$

$$\alpha FORK(j) = \{takes.0.j, drops.0.j, \dots, takes.4.j, drops.4.j\}$$

$$V = \left\langle \begin{matrix} PHIL(0), & PHIL(1), & PHIL(2), & PHIL(3), & PHIL(4) \\ FORK(0), & FORK(1), & FORK(2), & FORK(3), & FORK(4) \end{matrix} \right\rangle$$

where integer arithmetic is *modulo* 5.

The connection graph of this network is displayed in Figure 2.9. If we take the forks to be the resource processes, ordered by

$$FORK(4) > FORK(3) > FORK(2) > FORK(1) > FORK(0)$$

and the philosophers to be the user processes, we see that the Resource Allocation Protocol is adhered to by all processes except *PHIL(0)*. As explained in the Introduction section, deadlock is possible for this system, for instance, after trace

$$\langle takes.0.4, takes.1.0, takes.2.1, takes.4.3, takes.3.2 \rangle$$

Figure 2.9: Connection Graph for Dining Philosophers

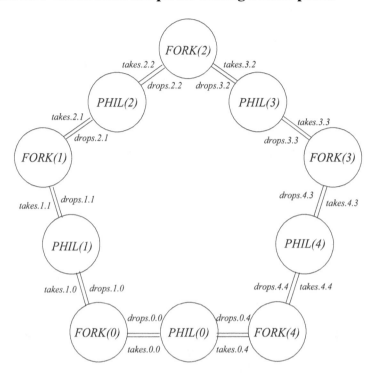

This is rectified by redefining *PHIL(0)* to pick up his right-hand fork first.

$$PHIL(0) = takes.0.4 \rightarrow takes.0.0 \rightarrow eats.0 \rightarrow$$
$$drops.0.4 \rightarrow drops.0.0 \rightarrow PHIL(0)$$

The resulting network is deadlock-free.

An Extended Protocol

The user processes will now be allowed to communicate with each other, so long as they do not attempt to do so while they are still holding any resources. The following result, inspired by an example from [Roscoe and Dathi 1986], will make it possible to build resources onto an existing deadlock-free network without introducing any risk of deadlock.

Rule 11 (Extended Resource Allocation Protocol) *Take a user-resource network V constructed from users $\{U_1, \ldots, U_N\}$ and resources $(\{R_1, \ldots, R_M\}, >)$. Suppose that no user process ever attempts to acquire a higher resource than any it already holds and never attempts* to communicate with another user process while holding a resource, i.e.,

$$\forall s \, : \, traces(U_i).$$

$$(s \downarrow claim_{ij} > s \downarrow release_{ij}) \wedge (R_k > R_j) \quad \Longrightarrow \quad s\,\widehat{}\,\langle claim_{ik} \rangle \notin traces(U_i)$$

$$(\exists j. \quad s \downarrow claim_{ij} > s \downarrow release_{ij}) \wedge l \neq i \quad \Longrightarrow \quad \forall e : \alpha U_i \cap \alpha U_l.$$

$$s\,\widehat{}\,\langle e \rangle \notin traces(U_i).$$

If the subnetwork of user processes $\langle U_1, \dots, U_N \rangle$ is deadlock-free, then the combined network of user processes and resource processes $\langle U_1, \dots, U_N, R_1, \dots, R_M \rangle$ is also deadlock-free.

Proof. Suppose that the conditions of the protocol are adhered to and also that the subnetwork of user processes $\langle U_1, \dots, U_N \rangle$ is deadlock-free, yet there is a deadlock state σ of the network. In this state, every process is blocked. First, we consider the possibility that in state σ no resource has been claimed, and therefore every resource is available to be claimed by any user process. It follows that each user process is only waiting to communicate with other user processes, *i.e.*, it is unable to perform any event outside the vocabulary of the subnetwork of user processes. So, the subnetwork $\langle U_1, \dots, U_N \rangle$ itself has a state, derived from σ, in which every process is blocked. This is a deadlock state, which contradicts our hypothesis.

So it must be the case that in state σ, at least one resource R_i has been claimed. It is therefore waiting to be released by some user process U_j. As U_j is currently holding resource R_i, it is not allowed to attempt communication with another user process, so it must be waiting to claim another resource. In this way, we can proceed to construct a cycle of ungranted requests, as was done in the proof of the basic Resource Allocation Protocol, leading to the same contradiction. We conclude that the network is deadlock-free☐.

Example – The Arm-Wrestling Philosophers

To illustrate this, we present a slight variation of the Dining Philosophers story, with arm-wrestling contests introduced to relieve the tedium of endless spaghetti eating and thinking. The philosophers are ranked according to seniority, given by

$$PHIL(4) > PHIL(3) > PHIL(2) > PHIL(1) > PHIL(0)$$

A philosopher may decide to eat some spaghetti or to challenge a senior philosopher to an arm-wrestling bout. Between meals, he is also prepared to accept a challenge from any of his juniors. The new CSP definitions for the philosophers are given as follows:

$$PHIL(0) = \left(\begin{array}{l} takes.0.4 \rightarrow takes.0.0 \rightarrow eats.0 \rightarrow \\ drops.0.4 \rightarrow drops.0.0 \rightarrow PHIL(0) \end{array} \right) \sqcap$$

$$(\sqcap_{i=1}^{4}\ wrestles.0.i \rightarrow PHIL(0))$$

$$PHIL(i) = \left(\left(\begin{array}{l} takes.i.i \rightarrow takes.i.(i-1) \rightarrow eats.i \rightarrow \\ drops.i.(i-1) \rightarrow drops.i.i \rightarrow PHIL(i) \end{array} \right) \sqcap \atop (\sqcap_{k=i+1}^{4}\ wrestles.i.k \rightarrow PHIL(i)) \right) \square$$

$$(\square_{k=0}^{i-1}\ wrestles.k.i \rightarrow PHIL(i)) \qquad\qquad i = 1,2,3$$

$$PHIL(4) = \left(\begin{array}{l} takes.4.4 \rightarrow takes.4.3 \rightarrow eats.4 \rightarrow \\ drops.4.3 \rightarrow drops.4.4 \rightarrow PHIL(4) \end{array} \right) \square$$

$$(\square_{k=0}^{3}\ wrestles.k.4 \rightarrow PHIL(4))$$

$$\alpha PHIL(i) = \{takes.i.i, takes.i.(i-1), eats.i, drops.i.(i-1), drops.i.i\}$$
$$\cup\ \{wrestles.i.k | k > i\} \cup \{wrestles.k.i | k < i\}$$

The subnetwork of philosophers is a simple example of a client-server network, where each philosopher interacts with his juniors as a server and his seniors as a client. It is easily shown to conform to the basic client-server protocol. Also, the Extended Resource Allocation Protocol is observed when it comes to the use of forks. Hence, the complete network of philosophers and forks is deadlock-free.

Figure 2.10: Arm-Wrestling Philosophers

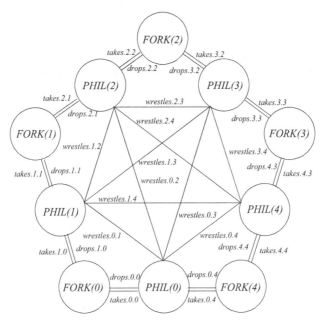

Example – A Parallel Database

The Extended Resource Allocation Protocol is generally applicable to parallel algorithms for manipulating and processing large datasets. For example, Figure 2.11 illustrates a simple design for a bank database. Each account is modelled as a resource process $ACCOUNT_j$. The user processes are configured as a *farm* network (consisting of a master and some slaves) to perform operations in parallel. Carrying out a transaction between two accounts requires that they be simultaneously held by a particular user process. There is clearly potential for deadlock here. Suppose that $SLAVE_p$ is told to move some money from $ACCOUNT_r$ to $ACCOUNT_s$, while at the same time $SLAVE_q$ is told to move some money from $ACCOUNT_s$ to $ACCOUNT_r$. If $SLAVE_p$ first opens $ACCOUNT_r$ and $SLAVE_q$ first opens $ACCOUNT_s$, they will become involved in a deadly embrace, which is likely to propagate throughout the system with disastrous consequences. The worst thing about this kind of deadlock is that it may take months or years of running time to appear, and so it might not be revealed by testing. The possibility of deadlock in this situation could be removed through placement of an ordering on the accounts (which may be arbitrary), followed by adherence to the Extended Resource Allocation Protocol. The system might be generalised to a multi-user distributed database, with more complicated transactions. As long as all the database records required for a transaction are known in advance, the protocol is easily obeyed by claiming them in ascending order. A similar approach to this is described in [Wolfson 1987].

In practice, deadlock is found to be a significant problem in multi-user databases. P. Marcino reports on an insurance database application that regularly experiences over a hundred deadlocks in a single day [Marcino 1995]. He points out that the deadlock issue was ignored during the design phase and only became apparent during initial testing. This is an all-too-common scenario. Much effort has been directed towards *deadlock-detection* algorithms [Knapp 1987]. Once a deadlock has been detected, steps can then be taken to remove it by 'rewinding' certain processes. It would seem to be much better programming practice to prevent deadlock from arising in the first place.

Figure 2.11: Bank Database System

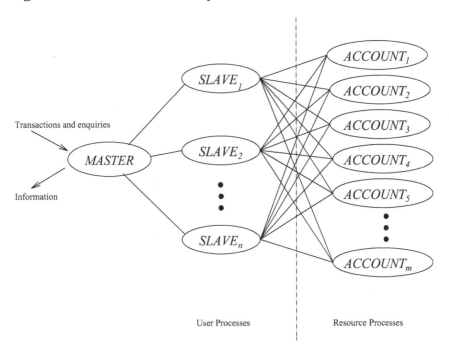

3

A TOOL FOR PROVING DEADLOCK FREEDOM

INTRODUCTION

This chapter describes the development of Deadlock Checker, a tool that checks for adherence to various design rules. It provides a vital safeguard against human error in their application.

As computer programs become increasingly vast and complex and are used for more and more safety-critical applications, the use of formal mathematical methods in their development is becoming crucial. Lives may depend on it. However, there are two important barriers to overcome. First, the large amount of work required in applying rigorous formal methods might seem infeasible. Second, computer programmers come from diverse backgrounds, and the level of mathematics involved will be off-putting to many and also increase the chance of error.

An important feature of the design rules in the previous chapter is that they are easy to describe in an informal, intuitive manner as well as having precise, formal statements. The algorithms employed by Deadlock Checker, described below, scale efficiently to networks of arbitrary size. The combination of simple design rules and efficient machine verification would seem to be a powerful weapon against deadlock. It offers a solution to both the problems described above in the specific context of building deadlock-free concurrent systems.

Deadlock Checker operates by testing the properties of individual CSP processes, or pairs of processes, within a network. This is done using *normal form* transition systems, which were devised by Roscoe for use in the refinement checking programme FDR. The act of normalising a transition system is described below. A method of checking failures specifications for individual processes and pairs of processes, using normalised transition systems, is then developed. This technique enables the automatic verification of adherence to the design rules of the previous chapter.

Deadlock Checker also implements a more general deadlock analysis algorithm. A network's state dependence digraph is defined where each vertex corresponds to a state of an individual process, and each arc represents a potential ungranted request between processes. It is shown that if the state dependence digraph is circuit-free, then the network is deadlock-free. This can be used to prove many useful networks deadlock-free, going beyond the bounds of the design rules. The programmer is allowed to be more adventurous and perhaps bend the rules. The drawback of this approach is that diagnostic messages are less informative.

3.1   NORMAL FORM TRANSITION SYSTEMS

The design rules that Deadlock Checker understands are defined by specifications in the *Failures-Divergences* model of CSP. The processes to be analysed are non-terminating, which means that they have failures sets of infinite size. These are clearly unwieldy objects to use for machine verification. Fortunately, Roscoe has developed a method for forming a unique, finite representation of any process that has a finite number of operational states [Roscoe 1994]. This is basically a hybrid form of its operational and denotational representations, which is called a *normal form transition system.* It is a digraph where each arc represents an event and each vertex a *composite state*, labelled with either a set of minimal acceptance sets or a flag $\perp$ to symbolise divergence.

Rather than offering a precise description, we shall outline the process of normalisation with the aid of a worked example. Consider a process P defined by the mutually recursive CSP equations

$$P = a \rightarrow b \rightarrow Q \sqcap c \rightarrow P$$
$$Q = a \rightarrow b \rightarrow P \sqcap c \rightarrow P$$

This process description is somewhat over-complicated for the behaviour it describes, as we shall soon see.

First, the syntax is parsed into a tree of operators acting on processes or pairs of processes. This, in turn, is converted into a state transition system using the inference rules for operational semantics. (See Section 1.3 for a description of this procedure.) Figure 3.1 illustrates the transition system for P. Recall that τ represents an internal decision – this is to cater for nondeterminism. States that have no τ transition event are described as *stable*, as no further internal activity is possible in those states.

Normalisation of a transition system is performed in three stages. First, a search is made for states from which an infinite series of hidden events is immediately possible (*i.e.*, states from which an indefinitely long walk of τ-labelled arcs can be constructed). Any such state is divergent and is labelled with ⊥. In our example, P is found to have no divergent state.

The second stage, called *pre-normalisation*, involves the elimination of τ arcs from the transition system and also results in a unique event labelling of arcs originating from any node.

First, the initial state is grouped together with any state that is reachable from there by performing a sequence of τ events. This group of states, which we shall call G_0, is collectively mapped to the initial state of the pre-normal state-transition system. Figure 3.2 shows how the initial state in the transition system for P (itself labelled P) is grouped with states labelled $a \rightarrow b \rightarrow Q \sqcap c \rightarrow P, a \rightarrow b \rightarrow Q$, and $c \rightarrow P$.

Figure 3.1: Transition System Resulting from Compilation

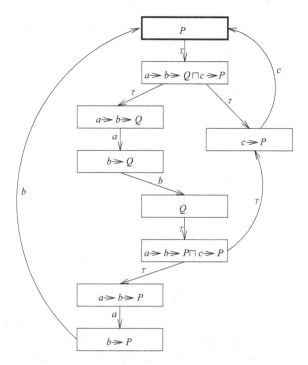

If G_0 contains any divergent state, then the new state is also labelled as divergent. Otherwise, the new state is labelled with a list of minimal acceptance sets. (Minimal acceptance sets are the complement of maximal refusal sets. Acceptance sets are used here only because they are typically smaller than refusal sets. The information carried is the same.) This is constructed by looking at all the stable states within G_0 and, for each one, the set of initial events that it offers. In Figure 3.2, the state labelled $a \to b \to Q$ offers $\{a\}$ and the state labelled $c \to P$ offers $\{c\}$, so the initial state in the new transition system is labelled with minimal acceptance sets $\{\{a\}, \{c\}\}$.

For each initial event x that is offered by states of G_0, apart from τ, a single transition is formed in the pre-normal transition system, leading to a new state constructed from the group of states reachable from states within G_0 by performing event x, possibly followed by a sequence of τ events. The new state is labelled using the technique described above. Each time a new group of states is formed, a check is made to see whether it has already been discovered. The activity terminates once there are no more new state groupings to be found. Figure 3.2 illustrates the entire pre-normalisation procedure for process P.

Figure 3.2: Pre-normalisation

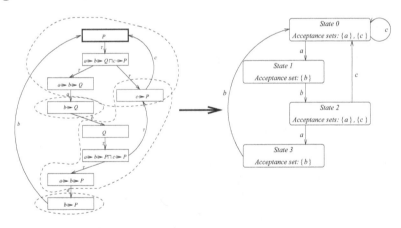

In the third stage, any states that are indistinguishable in terms of subsequent behaviour are combined to form a unique, compact normal form. Those states to be identified together are determined by first marking each state with *either* $\perp$ if it is divergent *or* its initial actions and minimal acceptance sets, and then computing the fixed point of the following sequence of equivalence relations:

- $S_1 \sim_0 S_2$ if, and only if, they have the same marking.
- $S_1 \sim_{n+1} S_2 \iff (S_1 \sim_n S_2) \wedge \forall S_1', S_2' \cdot (S_1 \xrightarrow{x} S_1' \wedge S_2 \xrightarrow{x} S_2' \implies S_1' \sim_n S_2')$

In our example, $\sim_0$ partitions the states of the pre-normal form into $\{\{0,2\}, \{1,3\}\}$. This partition is preserved by $\sim_1$, and so it represents the fixed point of $\sim_n$. This gives us the unique representation of P in Figure 3.3. Given that the initial state of this system is 0, it is simple to calculate the failures and divergences of P from this representation (by walking around the digraph).

Figure 3.3: Normal Form Transition System

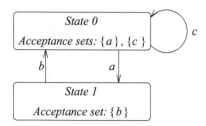

Let us be more precise about the relationship between the failures and divergences of a general process P and its normalised transition system N (if one exists). For every minimal divergent trace s of P, there will be a unique walk from the initial state σ_0 of N to a divergent state, with the transitions labelled according to s. Conversely, the labels of any walk from σ_0 to a divergent state of N form a minimal divergence of P. For every maximal failure (s, X) of P, such that s is not a divergence of P, there will be a unique walk labelled as s, going from σ_0 to a non-divergent state σ, which has a minimal acceptance set $\Sigma - X$. Conversely, for every walk labelled s from σ_0 to a nondivergent state σ, P has maximal failures $(s, \Sigma - A_1) \ldots (s, \Sigma - A_k)$, where $A_1 \ldots A_k$ are the minimal acceptance sets of state σ.

FDR uses normal form transition systems to check for the refinement relation $\sqsubseteq$ between two processes S and P. By stepping through the states of the two processes simultaneously, it is checked whether every possible behaviour of P is permitted by S [Roscoe 1994]. In particular, FDR is often used to prove deadlock freedom by checking for refinement against the worst possible deadlock-free process of a given alphabet. Full details of how it is used are given in [Formal Systems 1993]. It is a very general tool, but it runs into problems with large networks because of the exponential network state explosion as the number of processes increases.

3.2 DEADLOCK CHECKER

Deadlock Checker is implemented on top of FDR version 1.4, using the powerful functional programming language ML. (An excellent

Table 3.1 – Machine Readable CSP

Typeset CSP	ASCII CSP
$STOP$	STOP
$SKIP$	SKIP
$e \rightarrow P$	e -> P
$c!x \rightarrow P$	c!x -> P
$c?y \rightarrow P$	c?y -> P
$P \parallel[A \mid B]\parallel Q$	P [A||B] Q
$P \parallel\parallel Q$	P ||| Q
$P \sqcap Q$	P|~|Q
$P \square Q$	P [] Q
$\square_{i:A} P(i)$	[] i:A @ P(i)
$P \setminus A$	P \ A
$P \lhd (i = n) \rhd Q$	if i == n then P else Q

introduction is given to ML in [Paulson 1991].) It takes a network of CSP programs as input in the machine-readable syntax of [Scattergood 1992]. FDR is used to compile the network into a set of individual normal form transition systems – one for each process. These are then used for performing the local checks required to guarantee adherence to the various design paradigms and prove deadlock freedom. In this way, networks with very large numbers of states may rapidly be proven deadlock-free.

The main difference between machine-readable CSP and the algebraic form is that, in the former, the *type* of communication channels has to be explicitly defined using a pragma statement. The representation of various CSP operators in ASCII format is given in Table 3.1.

Comment lines beginning with --+ are used to specify to Deadlock Checker exactly which processes constitute the network to be analysed. There is no need to define the alphabets of these processes, as the compiler calculates them automatically (as being exactly those events that each process may ever perform). However, there are circumstances where one might wish explicitly to define the process alphabets, and this feature could be included in a future version of the program. Dijkstra's classic Dining Philosophers network may be defined as follows:

```
--- CSP process definitions

PHILNAMES = {0,1,2,3,4}
FORKNAMES = {0,1,2,3,4}
pragma channel eats:PHILNAMES
pragma channel takes, drops:PHILNAMES.FORKNAMES

PHIL(i) = takes.i.i -> takes.i.((i-1)%5)  -> eats.i ->
          drops.i.((i-1)\%5) -> drops.i.i -> PHIL(i)

FORK(i) = takes.i.i  -> drops.i.i -> FORK(i) []
  takes. ((i+1)%5).i -> drops. ((i+1)%5).i -> FORK(i)

--- Define network for Deadlock Checker

--+ PHIL(0),PHIL(1),PHIL(2),PHIL(3),PHIL(4)
--+ FORK(0),FORK(1),FORK(2),FORK(3),FORK(4)
```

This file, which is called `phils.csp`, is processed by Deadlock Checker into a file `phils.net` containing a set of normalised transition systems – one for each process in the network, by starting up the program and typing the following command:

compile "phils.csp" "phils.net";

Figure 3.4 illustrates the normal form transition systems for the Dining Philosophers network.

The interactive analysis may now proceed. First, we must type a command to put Deadlock Checker into interactive mode.

teletype ();
```
Welcome to Deadlock Checker
Command (h for help, q to quit):
```

Typing *h* summons the following menu of commands:

```
h           - help: display this menu
l <file> - load network file
n           - display list of networks in memory
s <name> - select network
c           - display currently selected network
p           - display list of processes in current network
d           - decompose network analysis
v           - check for acyclic deadlock freedom
              (SDD algorithm)
x           - check for acyclic deadlock freedom
              (CSDD algorithm)
o           - check for deadlock in cyclic-po network
w           - check for deadlock in client-server network
a           - check for resource allocation protocol
r           - restrict network to its vocabulary
t           - test for livelock-freedom (Roscoe's rule)
```

We load the compiled network definition as follows:

```
Command (h for help, q to quit):l phils.net
```

Figure 3.4: Normal Form Transition Systems for Dining Philosophers

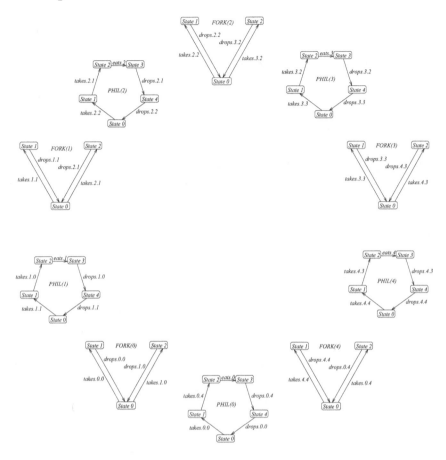

Then, we instruct Deadlock Checker to check for adherence to the Resource Allocation Protocol.

```
Command (h for help, q to quit):a
Network phils.net is busy
Network phils.net is triple-disjoint
Process FORK(4) acts as a resource
Process FORK(3) acts as a resource
Process FORK(2) acts as a resource
Process FORK(1) acts as a resource
Process FORK(0) acts as a resource
Process PHIL(4) is not a resource
User process PHIL(4) obeys resource allocation protocol
User process PHIL(3) obeys resource allocation protocol
User process PHIL(2) obeys resource allocation protocol
User process PHIL(1) obeys resource allocation protocol
User process PHIL(0) claims resource FORK(4) still holding FORK(0)
```

This network is not deadlock-free, and Deadlock Checker reveals the problem. The techniques used by Deadlock Checker to perform this analysis, and the other commands, will now be explained in detail. Further details are also to be found in [Martin 1995].

3.3   CHECKING ADHERENCE TO DESIGN RULES

In this section, we shall give details of the various algorithms employed by Deadlock Checker to test adherence to design rules. These algorithms will be illustrated with examples. We shall also estimate their time complexity as a function of n, where n is the number of processes in the network, unless otherwise stated.

Checking Network Prerequisites
Recall that our networks must be *triple-disjoint*, meaning that no event may be shared by more than two processes, and *busy*, meaning that each process must be deadlock-free, divergence-free, and non-terminating. The property of triple-disjointedness can be established by the following algorithm:

1. Assume that the events in the network $\langle P_1, \dots, P_n \rangle$ are numbered from 1 to m (we use the integer keys that FDR assigns to each event during compilation). Set up two arrays, *first* and *second*, with dimension m, which are initially 'undefined'.
2. Scan the alphabet of each process P_i in turn. For each event $e \in \alpha P_i$, if *first*(e) is undefined, then set

$$first(e) := i$$

otherwise if *second*(e) is undefined, then set

$$second(e) := i$$

otherwise halt, because event e lies in the alphabet of three processes, and so the network is not triple disjoint.

If we assume that the average number of events in the alphabet of each process remains fixed as the number of processes in the network, n, increases, then the time complexity is $O(n)$.

'Business' is also checked in $O(n)$ time if we assume that the average number of states of each process remains roughly constant as n increases. We simply check every state of every process to make sure that it is not labelled as divergent and also does not have the empty set as a minimal acceptance set.

The prototype version of Deadlock Checker is programmed using only the standard core of ML. As this has no imperative arrays, the program does not achieve the theoretical efficiency of certain algorithms that it implements.

Checking Trace and Refusal Specifications

Any information about failures and divergences of a process may be extracted from its normalised transition system. Specifications on refusal sets are easy to check because all the required information may be deduced from the list of minimal acceptance sets stored at each vertex, and each vertex only needs to be looked at once. However, a trace specification could potentially lead to an infinite search if not carefully stated.

Consider the specification

$$\forall s \in traces(P). \ \ (s \downarrow b + 4) \geq 2(s \downarrow a) \geq s \downarrow b$$

Starting at the initial state of P, we might search through the transition digraph, keeping a record of the current trace, and checking every possible trace for $s \downarrow a$ and $s \downarrow b$. This search might never terminate for a component of a busy network.

There is a much better approach to this problem as follows. We write our specification like this

$$\forall s \in traces(P).4 \geq 2(s \downarrow a) - s \downarrow b \geq 0$$

Then, we define an *incremental* trace function f as follows:

$$f(\langle \rangle) = 0$$

$$f(s^\frown \langle x \rangle) = \begin{cases} f(s) + 2 & if \ \ x = a \\ f(s) - 1 & if \ \ x = b \\ f(s) & otherwise \end{cases}$$

It is clear that

$$f(s) = 2(s \downarrow a) - s \downarrow b$$

We start an exhaustive search through the transition system for pairs of the form (σ, v), where σ is a state and v is a possible value of $f(s)$ at that state. The search terminates either when there are no new such pairs to be found or if we find a pair for which $\neg(4 \geq v \geq 0)$.

There are two reasons why this approach is better. First, we have defined our variant function, f, in an incremental way, which means that we do not need to store any information about traces. The value of $f(s)$ at each point in the search can be calculated purely from the information stored at the previous point. Second, we have converted an endless search into one that is guaranteed to terminate due to the bounds placed on the range of f.

This technique can be extended to a network of two processes $\langle P, Q \rangle$ and a specification on network states $(s, \langle X_P, X_Q \rangle)$. We assume that the specification is expressed as a predicate

$$PRED(f_1(s), \dots, f_n(s), X_P, X_Q)$$

involving a number of incremental trace functions f_i and maximal refusal sets X_P and X_Q of P and Q.

Two sets of records are maintained: *pending* and *done*. Each record is of the form $(\sigma_P, \sigma_Q, v_1, \dots, v_n)$, where (σ_P, σ_Q) is a pair of normal form states in which P and Q may simultaneously rest, and each v_i is the value of $f_i(s)$ for a corresponding trace s. The algorithm proceeds as follows:

1. Initially, *pending* consists of a single record corresponding to the original state of the system, and *done* is empty.

$$pending := \{(0, 0, f_1(\langle \rangle), \dots, f_n(\langle \rangle))\}$$
$$done := \{\}$$

2. Take a new record from *pending* to be processed.

$$r := (\sigma_P, \sigma_Q, v_1, \dots, v_n) \in pending$$
$$pending := pending - \{r\}$$

3. Now, check whether record r satisfies the specification. Suppose that σ_P has a set A of minimal acceptance sets and σ_Q has a set B of minimal acceptance sets. If $\exists a : A, b : B. \neg PRED(v_1, \dots, v_n, \alpha P - a, \alpha Q - b)$, then halt. (The specification is *not* satisfied.) Otherwise

$$done := done \cup \{r\}$$

4. Now, construct the set *new* of successor records of r by considering every transition that is possible for $PAR(\langle P, Q \rangle)$ from state pair (σ_P, σ_Q). Assume that r corresponds to some trace s of $PAR(\langle P, Q \rangle)$. Then,

$$new := \bigcup \left\{ \begin{array}{l} (\sigma'_P, \sigma_Q, f_1(s^\frown\langle x\rangle), \dots, f_n(s^\frown\langle x\rangle)) | \\ \quad x \in \alpha P - \alpha Q \wedge \sigma_P \xrightarrow{x} \sigma'_P \end{array} \right\}$$
$$\cup \left\{ \begin{array}{l} (\sigma_P, \sigma'_Q, f_1(s^\frown\langle x\rangle), \dots, f_n(s^\frown\langle x\rangle)) | \\ \quad x \in \alpha Q - \alpha P \wedge \sigma_Q \xrightarrow{x} \sigma'_Q \end{array} \right\}$$
$$\cup \left\{ \begin{array}{l} (\sigma'_P, \sigma'_Q, f_1(s^\frown\langle x\rangle), \dots, f_n(s^\frown\langle x\rangle)) | \\ \quad x \in \alpha P \cap \alpha Q \wedge \sigma_P \xrightarrow{x} \sigma'_P \wedge \sigma_Q \xrightarrow{x} \sigma'_Q \end{array} \right\}$$

Although we have not stored any record of a value of s that corresponds to r, it is not actually required in order to perform this calculation due to the incremental method of defining the various trace functions.

5. Now, we eliminate records from *new* that have already been processed and merge the remainder into *pending*.

$$pending := pending \cup (new - done)$$

6. If *pending* = { }, then halt. (The specification is satisfied.) Otherwise, return to step 2.

This algorithm is not certain to terminate for every given set of incremental trace functions f_i and predicate *PRED*. But if there is a finite range of values for each f_i outside which the satisfaction of *PRED* is impossible, then termination is guaranteed for any network $\langle P, Q \rangle$.

The following example is included in order to illustrate this technique. Consider the network $V = \langle LEFT, RIGHT \rangle$ with the following process definitions:

$$LEFT = in \rightarrow mid \rightarrow LEFT$$
$$\alpha LEFT = \{in, mid\}$$

$$RIGHT = mid \rightarrow out \rightarrow RIGHT$$
$$\alpha RIGHT = \{mid, out\}$$

Suppose we wish to prove that the following trace specification is satisfied by $PAR(V)$.

$$2 \geq s \downarrow in - s \downarrow out \geq 0$$

V is an abstract representation of a double buffer, which inputs information on channel *in* and outputs it on channel *out*. The specification simply states that the number of messages held in the buffer at any given time lies between nought and two inclusive.

We proceed by defining an incremental trace function f as follows:

$$f(\langle \rangle) = 0$$

$$f(s^\frown \langle x \rangle) = \begin{cases} f(s) + 1 & if \quad x = in \\ f(s) - 1 & if \quad x = out \\ f(s) & otherwise \end{cases}$$

It is clear that

$$f(s) = s \downarrow in - s \downarrow out$$

In this case, our predicate function *PRED* is given by

$$PRED(f(s)) = (2 \geq f(s) \geq 0)$$

Normal form state transition systems for the network V are shown in Figure 3.5. We now proceed to form an exhaustive set of records of the form

$$(\sigma_{LEFT}, \sigma_{RIGHT}, val)$$

consisting of a state of process *LEFT*, a corresponding state of process *RIGHT*, and a possible value for $f(s)$ when the processes are in those states.

Figure 3.5: Normal Form Transition Systems for Two-Place Buffer

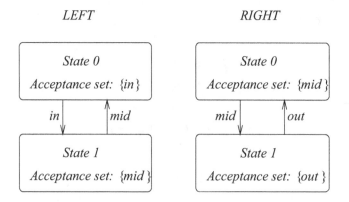

The search proceeds as follows. First, we have

$$pending = \{(0,0,0)\}, \quad done = \{\}$$

Check $(0,0,0)$; possible transition is *in*; leads to record: $(1,0,1)$. Now we have

$$pending = \{(1,0,1)\}, \quad done = \{(0,0,0)\}$$

Check $(1,0,1)$; possible transition is *mid*; leads to record: $(0,1,1)$. Now we have

$$pending = \{(0,1,1)\}, \quad done = \{(0,0,0),(1,0,1)\}$$

Check $(0,1,1)$; possible transitions are *in, out*; lead to records: $(1,1,2)$, $(0,0,0)$. Now we have

$$pending = \{(1,1,2)\}, \quad done = \{(0,0,0),(1,0,1),(0,1,1)\}$$

Check $(1,1,2)$; possible transition is *out*; leads to record: $(1,0,1)$. Now we have

$$pending = \{\}, \quad done = \{(0,0,0), (1,0,1), (0,1,1), (1,1,2)\}$$

The search is now complete. Every record that was found satisfies the original specification, and we shall conclude that it is satisfied by *PAR(V)*. This is rather a bold claim given that the set of traces of *PAR(V)* is infinite and we have only examined four cases. But it may be justified by using induction on traces, as follows:

Every trace s of *PAR(V)* corresponds to a unique pair of normal form states

$$(\sigma_{LEFT}, \sigma_{RIGHT})$$

These are found by constructing the unique walk in the normal form transition system of *LEFT* with labels $s \upharpoonright \alpha LEFT$, and the unique walk in the normal form transition system of *RIGHT* with labels $s \upharpoonright \alpha RIGHT$. We shall call this state pair

$$(\sigma_{LEFT}(s), \sigma_{RIGHT}(s))$$

Now suppose that for a certain trace t, we know that record

$$(\sigma_{LEFT}(t), \sigma_{RIGHT}(t), f(t))$$

lies in set *done*, constructed above. Now consider a trace $t^\frown \langle x \rangle$ of V. This corresponds to a state pair

$$(\sigma_{LEFT}(t^\frown \langle x \rangle), \sigma_{RIGHT}(t^\frown \langle x \rangle))$$

which must be reachable from $(\sigma_{LEFT}, \sigma_{RIGHT})$ by one or both of the processes performing event x. It follows that record

$$(\sigma_{LEFT}(t^\frown \langle x \rangle), \sigma_{RIGHT}(t^\frown \langle x \rangle), f(t^\frown \langle x \rangle))$$

must also lie in set *done*, due to the incremental way in which this set was constructed.

We actually know that

$$(\sigma_{LEFT}(\langle \rangle), \sigma_{RIGHT}(\langle \rangle), f(\langle \rangle)) = (0,0,0) \in done$$

because this is the record that was used to start the search. Hence, by induction, *every* trace s of V is represented in *done* by a record of the form

$$(\sigma_{LEFT}(s), \sigma_{RIGHT}(s), f(s))$$

So, we conclude that the original specification is satisfied by all traces of $PAR(V)$.

Although this proof technique is tedious for humans, it is very easy to automate on a computer. It would be feasible to extend the technique to networks of more than two processes, but due to the exponential state explosion as networks grow larger, this would have limited potential in practice.

Note that, for individual processes, it is often feasible to perform this kind of specification check using FDR directly. To prove that a process P satisfies some specification, one constructs a process S that is the worst possible process that satisfies the specification and then shows that $P \sqsupseteq S$. However, specifications of networks of two processes that involve the refusal sets of individual processes, such as the formal statement of conflict-freedom, cannot be checked directly using FDR.

Resource Allocation Protocol

Deadlock Checker includes a check for adherence to the Extended Resource Allocation Protocol. This depends on the processes that constitute the network being presented in a particular order. The network is assumed to consist of a sequence of user processes $\langle U_1, \ldots, U_M \rangle$, followed by an ordered sequence of resource processes $\langle R_1, \ldots, R_N \rangle$. Observe that in the example of the Dining Philosophers network (page 73), the processes are presented in the following order (which conforms to this requirement):

```
--+ PHIL(0),PHIL(1),PHIL(2),PHIL(3),PHIL(4)
--+ FORK(0),FORK(1),FORK(2),FORK(3),FORK(4)
```

The analysis proceeds in two stages. The first stage is to start from the end of the list and work backwards to see how many processes behave as resources.

Checking that a process P behaves as a resource relies on the fact that the normal form transition system of a resource process has a very specific form. Consider a general resource process

$$R = \square_{i=1}^{k} c_i \rightarrow r_i \rightarrow R$$

The normal form transition system for this process is shown in Figure 3.6. It has an initial state representing the situation where the resource has not been 'claimed', plus one state for each claim channel c_i, representing the state of having been claimed on that channel.

Figure 3.6: Normal Form Transition System for General Resource Process

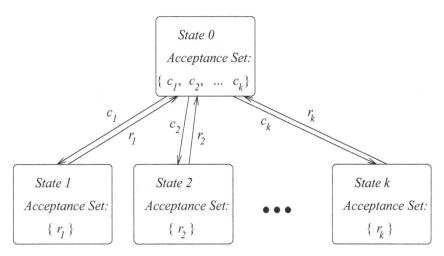

To establish whether a given process P is of this form involves first attempting to split its alphabet into a set of *claim-release* pairs $\{(c_1, r_1), \dots (c_k, r_k)\}$. The initial state of P should have a single minimal acceptance set $\{c_1, \dots, c_k\}$ equal to the set of initial events of P. Then, for each c_i, there should be a transition to a state S_i with a single minimal acceptance set $\{r_i\}$ and a single transition back to the initial state of P. Each of the r_i must be distinct and different from all the c_i.

If this splitting of αP proves successful, it must then be checked that each of the claim-release pairs consists of events from the alphabet of a process before P in the network list. Also, no two event pairs should match the same process. If this is so, P is taken to be a valid resource process. At the same time, a list of claim-release pairs, $cr\_list(U)$, is constructed for each user process U, consisting of records of the form $((c, r), n)$, where (c, r) is a claim-release pair and n is a resource number (taken as the numeric order of the resource in the network). (Note that we have relaxed the condition that each resource needs to make itself available to every user process. A resource may be private to a particular subset of users.)

Performing this check on the normal form transition system for process $FORK(4)$ (see Figure 3.4) results in splitting up its alphabet into two pairs

$$\{(takes.4.4, drops.4.4), (takes.0.4, drops.0.4)\}$$

It is then found that

$$\{takes.4.4, drops.4.4\} \subseteq \alpha PHIL(4)$$
$$\{takes.0.4, drops.0.4\} \subseteq \alpha PHIL(0)$$

So, it is concluded that *FORK(4)* is a resource.

As soon as a process is discovered that does not behave as a resource, it is taken to be a user process, along with all the processes that precede it in the network ordering. In the case of the Dining Philosophers, the first non-resource process discovered is *PHIL(4)*. Each user process must then be checked for adherence to the Extended Resource Allocation Protocol. This protocol was defined formally using failures specifications on page 63. We need to check that each user process U communicates with its resources in alternating sequence on each (c, r) pair in $cr\_list(U)$. Also, it attempts only to claim resources ordered below those that it already holds and never attempts to communicate with another user while holding a resource. This is achieved by casting the specification in terms of incremental trace functions and then using the technique described on page 77, as follows:

Let

$$cr\_list(U) = \langle ((c_1, r_1), n_1), \dots, ((c_k, r_k), n_k) \rangle$$

Then, for each $i \in \{1, \dots, k\}$ define

$$f_i(s) = s \downarrow c_i - s \downarrow r_i$$

Incrementally, this is written as

$$f_i(\langle \rangle) = 0$$

$$f_i(s^\frown \langle x \rangle) = \begin{cases} f_i(s) + 1 & \text{if} \quad x = c_i \\ f_i(s) - 1 & \text{if} \quad x = r_i \\ f_i(s) & \text{otherwise} \end{cases}$$

Function $f_i(s)$ should take the value *1* whenever user U is holding resource n_i and otherwise take the value *0*. In this case, rather than examining the minimal acceptance sets of U after trace s, we need to look at its initial events I. These are available as the transition events that are possible from the normal form state of U that corresponds to s. We define

$$PRED(f_1(s), \dots, f_k(s), I) = \left(\begin{array}{c} \forall j : \{1, \dots, k\}.(1 \ge f_j(s) \ge 0) \wedge \\ \left(f_j(s) = 1 \Rightarrow \left(\begin{array}{c} (\forall i.c_i \in I \Rightarrow n_i < n_j) \wedge \\ (\forall U' \ne U.I \cap \alpha U' = \{\}) \end{array} \right) \right) \end{array} \right)$$

If this specification check succeeds for each user process, then the deadlock analysis is reduced to the subnetwork $\langle U_1, \dots U_M \rangle$, which must be analysed by other means. It may well be that the user processes have disjoint alphabets, in which case no further analysis is required.

It is important to note a minor flaw in the part of the algorithm that identifies resource processes. It is possible that a network could contain one or more processes that are intended to be treated as users but that never actually use any resources and appear to behave like resources themselves. These could be identified as such in the searching process described above, which could then lead to a valid deadlock-free network being rejected. This is very unlikely to occur in practice. The problem could be avoided by modifying Deadlock Checker to insist that resource processes be explicitly labelled as such, but as this would cause unnecessary inconvenience in the vast majority of cases, it has not been done.

Complexity

We shall continue to assume that as the number of processes in a network, n, increases, the number of states and events of each process remains approximately fixed. This means that the time taken to perform any local analysis of an individual process, or pairs of neighbouring processes, can be assumed to be independent of the size of the network.

Let us consider the algorithm for checking the Resource Allocation Protocol. We assume that the proportion of user processes to resource processes remains fixed as n grows. Starting at the end of the network list, the claim-release channel pairs for each resource process discovered need to be matched with the alphabet of the process that precedes it. Each matching operation can be done in constant time by making use of the two arrays *first* and *second*, indexed by events in αV, which were set up in order to verify triple-disjointedness (page 76). So, the entire matching process is $O(n)$. All the other checking performed is local to a process, and so $O(n)$ for the network as a whole (by the above assumptions). This gives us an overall complexity of $O(n)$.

Cyclic Processes

To analyse a network purporting to be cyclic-PO, we need to check that each process communicates cyclically on its channels according to some partial order, for which we construct the Hasse digraph. This is the minimal representation of a partial order; it has a vertex for each element of the partial order and an arc xy whenever element y is *directly* below x, i.e.,

$$ x > y \quad \wedge \quad \nexists z. x > z > y $$

Then, to prove deadlock freedom, we must show that the union of the Hasse digraphs, which we call the *channel dependence digraph,* contains no circuit.

Recall that we formally defined the cyclic-po process *CYCLIC-PO* $(X, >)$, which communicates on the set of channels X, partially ordered by $>$, as follows:

$$CYCLIC\text{-}PO(X, >) = C2(X, \{\}, >)$$
$$C2(X, DONE, >) = C2(X, \{\}, >)$$
$$\lhd DONE = X \rhd$$
$$\square_{x:mins(X-DONE,>)}x \rightarrow C2(X, DONE \cup \{x\}, >)$$

where $mins(Y, >)$ is defined as the minimal elements of subset Y of X, given by

$$mins(Y, >) = \{y \in Y | \not\exists z \in Y. \quad y > z\}$$

It can be shown that this definition is unchanged when $(X, >)$ is replaced with its Hasse digraph.

For verifying that a process P is cyclic and extracting its Hasse channel ordering, a two-pass algorithm is employed as follows. The first pass tries to extract a Hasse digraph on the assumption that the process is indeed *cyclic*. In each state s of the normal form transition system of P, we look at every transition (e, s') that does not take us back to the initial state of P. If an event e' is possible in state s' that was not possible in state s, we assume that $e' > e$. When this first stage is complete, we will have constructed a relation $>$ on the channels of P. If P is cyclic-PO, this will actually be the Hasse digraph of its channel ordering. This is because whenever a cyclic-PO process performs an event e and then immediately becomes ready to perform event e', without having completed a cycle, e' must be directly above e in the channel ordering. If P is not cyclic-PO, the relation that we have constructed will be meaningless.

If the $>$ relation contains a cycle $c_1 > ... > c_k > c_1$, we can eliminate P straight away. Otherwise, we must now check whether the behaviour of P adheres exactly to $CYCLIC\text{-}PO(\alpha P, >)$. This relies on the normal form transition system of the latter having a very specific form. Each state corresponds to the process $C2(\alpha P, DONE, >)$ for a particular set of events $DONE$. We perform the check using a depth-first search (see Appendix B), starting from the initial state of P. For each state of P that we visit, we maintain a record of the events that have been performed to arrive there, and we call this set $DONE$. We then check that the immediate behaviour at each state, as given by its acceptance sets and transition events, conforms to that of $C2(X, DONE, >)$.

We also check that *DONE* is consistent when a state is visited more than once. Whenever the initial state is revisited, *DONE* should be equal to αP. This second pass can only succeed if P is cyclic-po with ordering >.

If every process in the network is found to be cyclic-PO, the Hasse digraphs of their channel orderings are aggregated into a global channel dependence digraph. We know from Theorem 7, page 44, that the network is deadlock-free if, and only if, there is no circuit in the $\triangleright$ relation

$$c_1 \triangleright c_2 \triangleright ... \triangleright c_m \triangleright c_1$$

Now $\triangleright$ is the union of the full channel orderings of each process in the network, and so the channel dependency digraph is a subset of $\triangleright$. However, it is a subset that carries all the vital information, and it may easily be shown that the channel dependency digraph contains a circuit if, and only if, $\triangleright$ contains a cycle. It follows that the network is deadlock-free if, and only if, there is no circuit in the channel dependency digraph. This is checked using the DFS algorithm.

To demonstrate the use of this tool, we recall the toroidal cellular array. This is coded in machine-readable CSP as follows:

```
n=4
indices = {0,1,2,3}
pragma channel e:indices.indices.{left,up,right,down}

CELL(i,j) = if ((i+j)%2==0) then LEFT(i, j) else RIGHT(i, j)

LEFT(i,j) = e.i.j.left -> e.((i-1)%n).j.right -> UP(i, j) []
            e.((i-1)%n).j.right -> e.i.j.left   -> UP(i, j)

UP(i,j) = e.i.j.up -> e.i.((j-1)%n).down -> RIGHT(i, j) []
          e.i.((j-1)%n).down -> e.i.j.up -> RIGHT(i, j)

RIGHT(i,j) = e.i.j.right -> e.((i+1)%n).j.left -> DOWN(i, j) []
             e.((i+1)%n).j.left -> e.i.j.right -> DOWN(i, j)

DOWN(i,j) = e.i.j.down -> e.i.((j+1)%n).up -> LEFT(i, j) []
            e.i.((j+1)%n).up -> e.i.j.down -> LEFT(i, j)

--+ CELL(0,0),CELL(1,0),CELL(2,0),CELL(3,0)
--+ CELL(0,1),CELL(1,1),CELL(2,1),CELL(3,1)
--+ CELL(0,2),CELL(1,2),CELL(2,2),CELL(3,2)
--+ CELL(0,3),CELL(1,3),CELL(2,3),CELL(3,3)
```

Each process is cyclic and communicates with each of its neighbours in turn. (Note that the interleaving construct has been algebraically transformed into an external choice. This is due to a syntax restriction placed on CSP by FDR 1.4.) Deadlock should be avoided because alternate cells commence with different orientations. The Hasse digraph and normal form state transition system for process *CELL(0,0)* are illustrated in Figure 3.7.

Figure 3.7: Hasse Digraph and Normal Form Transition System for *CELL(0,0)*

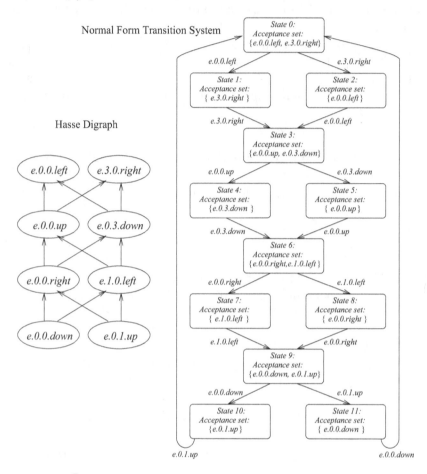

We load the compiled network definitions and check for adherence to the cyclic-PO protocol.

```
Command (h for help, q to quit): l torus.net
Command (h for help, q to quit): o
```

For each process in the network, a report like this one is returned

```
Process CELL(0,0) is cyclic-PO:
  (e.0.0.up    > e.3.0.right), (e.0.3.down > e.3.0.right),
  (e.0.0.up    > e.0.0.left ), (e.0.3.down > e.0.0.left ),
  (e.0.0.right > e.0.3.down ), (e.1.0.left > e.0.3.down ),
  (e.0.0.right > e.0.0.up   ), (e.1.0.left > e.0.0.up   ),
  (e.0.0.down  > e.1.0.left ), (e.0.1.up   > e.1.0.left ),
  (e.0.0.down  > e.0.0.right), (e.0.1.up   > e.0.0.right)
```

The program then checks for circuits in the channel dependency digraph, and finding none reports

```
Network torus.net is deadlock-free
```

88

If we change the dimensions of the toroidal array to 5×5, it turns out that the network will deadlock, as is revealed by Deadlock Checker in the following way:

```
Found closed trail of dependent channels:
<e.4.4.right,e.4.4.up,e.4.3.right,e.0.4.up,e.4.4.right>
Network torus5.net deadlocks
```

When deadlock has been identified, the reason behind it is always reported.

The algorithm for checking cyclic-PO networks involves local checking of each process to establish its channel ordering, which is $O(n)$, plus a check for circuits in the channel dependence digraph. We can assume that the number of edges in this graph grows proportionally to n by taking the number of edges in the Hasse digraph of each process to be independent of n. Checking for circuits can be performed in linear time with the DFS algorithm. So, the cyclic-PO network check can be done with $O(n)$ complexity.

Client-Server Protocol

Deadlock Checker contains a tool for verifying that a network has been implemented according to the basic client-server protocol (described on page 49). There are two phases to the method employed. First, the program attempts to identify the client and server channel bundles of each process in the network. For this to be feasible, the order in which the processes are supplied in the network is significant. A process should communicate with those before it as a server and those after it as a client. This would guarantee that the client-server digraph would be free of circuits. Second, the program checks for conformance to the basic CSP specifications using the channel bundles that have just been calculated.

The first part of the algorithm, which calculates the channel bundles of each process, has limitations. It will not succeed in correctly identifying client and server channel bundles for certain valid basic client-server networks. There are two possible reasons for this. The first is that it is assumed that there is no *polling* on client or server channels. (By polling, we mean a process of communicating on a channel when in an unstable state, for instance, if it is waiting for some concealed time-out event.) The second, which is less important, is only likely to arise due to a coding error and is described below.

However, the method for verifying that a process with *given* client and server channel bundles obeys the basic protocol is precise and will work for any basic client-server network. It is a simple application of the specification checking technique described on page 77.

To assist with explaining this algorithm, we shall consider its application to the simple process farm described in Chapter 2. The machine-readable description of this network is as follows:

```
iset = {0,1,2,3,4}
jset = {0,1,2}
pragma channel a,b: iset.jset
pragma channel c,d: iset

WORKER(i,j) = a.i.j -> b.i.j -> WORKER(i,j)

FOREMAN(i) = [] j:jset @ (a.i.j -> c.i ->
             d.i -> b.i.j -> FOREMAN(i))

FARMER = [] i:iset @ (c.i -> d.i -> FARMER)

--+ WORKER(0,0),WORKER(0,1),WORKER(0,2),
--+ WORKER(1,0),WORKER(1,1),WORKER(1,2),
--+ WORKER(2,0),WORKER(2,1),WORKER(2,2),
--+ WORKER(3,0),WORKER(3,1),WORKER(3,2),
--+ WORKER(4,0),WORKER(4,1),WORKER(4,2),
--+ FOREMAN(0),FOREMAN(1),FOREMAN(2),FOREMAN(3),FOREMAN(4)
--+ FARMER
```

The normal form transition system for process *FOREMAN(0)* is illustrated in Figure 3.8.

To establish the client and server bundles of a network, the following steps are performed:

Figure 3.8: Normal Form Transition System for *FOREMAN(0)*

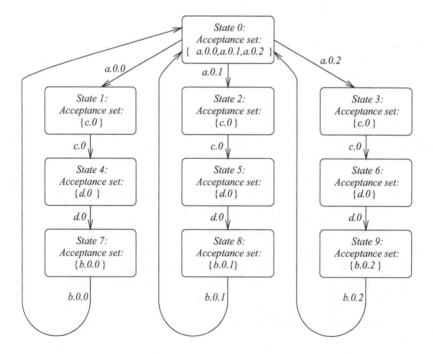

1. For each process P in the network list, the set of channels that it uses to communicate with predecessors in the list is compiled: $B(P)$. This should represent the union of channels in P's server bundles, which must be disjoint, i.e., there is no channel shared by two server bundles.

   For process $FOREMAN(0)$, we find that

   $$B(FOREMAN(0)) = \{a.0.0, b.0.0, a.0.1, b.0.1, a.0.2, b.0.2\}$$

2. For each process P, we start at its initial state and perform a depth-first search until we find a state S where P can accept communication on a server channel, *i.e.*, there is a minimal acceptance set A that intersects with $B(P)$. By rule **(b)** of the basic client-server definition, $A \cap B(P)$ should consist of all the server requisition and drip channels of P. (This assumes that there is no communication by polling, in which case a server requisition or drip might have already occurred without having appeared in a minimal acceptance set.)

   Process $FOREMAN(0)$ accepts communication on server channels while in its initial state, where it has a minimal acceptance set $A = \{a.0.0, a.0.1, a.0.2\}$.

3. For each channel c in $A \cap B(P)$, we take the corresponding transition from state S to a new state S'. We then construct a server bundle from c by performing a DFS, rooted at S', to find a successor state where P has a transition on some server channel c'. If c' lies in $A \cap B(P)$, *i.e.*, it is a requisition or a drip, then c must be a drip; otherwise, (c, c') is a requisition-acknowledge bundle. If, however, the DFS terminates without finding another communication on a server channel, it means that the process might never be able to communicate on a server channel again after performing event c. In this case, we take c to be a drip channel. It is theoretically possible that this is incorrect and that c is actually a requisition channel, but in practice, this is most likely to be a coding error in process P.

   Applying this step to $FOREMAN(0)$ involves performing DFS searches rooted at states 1, 2, and 3 to find the next state where a server event may be performed. In each case, a new server event is discovered (in states 7, 8, and 9, respectively) which results in the construction of three requisition-acknowledge bundles for the process, as follows:

   $$servers(FOREMAN(0)) = \{\langle a.0.0, b.0.0 \rangle, \langle a.0.1, b.0.1 \rangle, \\ \langle a.0.2, b.0.2 \rangle\}$$

4. Having calculated the server channel bundles of a process P, we must check that they are disjoint and that their union is $B(P)$. Both of these properties are clearly satisfied for FOREMAN(0).

5. The next step is to assign each server bundle of P to another process as a client bundle. This is done by checking that the channels that form each server bundle belong to the alphabet of some preceding process in the list. If there is any server bundle that cannot be matched in this way, then something is wrong with the network being checked. The three server bundles of FOREMAN(0) are allocated as client bundles to WORKER(0,0), WORKER(0,1), and WORKER(0,2), respectively.

If each stage has been successful, then we shall have calculated a set of client and server bundles for each process, which can now be checked against the basic protocol. However, it is possible that this procedure might have failed even if the processes were valid, for the two reasons given above. It is important to make it clear that this limitation could never result in Deadlock Checker passing a network as being deadlock-free when it actually deadlocks. The restriction could easily be overcome by requiring the client and server bundles to be explicitly defined in the original CSP network script, although this would be inconvenient to the user. Perhaps both options should be offered in a future version of Deadlock Checker. (However, the more general SDD algorithm, which will be described below, can correctly identify deadlock freedom for any basic client-server network, regardless of the order in which the processes are supplied.)

The second phase, which is checking that each process obeys the basic client-server protocol, is a straightforward application of the CSP specification checking technique described on page 76, using the formal definition of the rules of the basic client-server protocol, recast in terms of incremental trace functions.

To demonstrate the tool in action again, here is the analysis of the simple process farm.

```
Command (h for help, q to quit):l farm.net
Command (h for help, q to quit):w
```

For each process in the network, a report of the following form is returned:

```
Process FOREMAN(0) obeys client-server protocol:
  clients(FOREMAN(0)) = {<c.0,d.0>}
  servers(FOREMAN(0)) = {<a.0.0,b.0.0>,<a.0.1,b.0.1>,<a.0.2,b.0.2>}
```

As each process satisfies the protocol, the program concludes that the network will never deadlock.

```
Network farm.net is deadlock-free
```

We shall now estimate the complexity of the algorithm for checking adherence to the basic client-server protocol with the usual assumptions about the number of states and events of each process. Calculating the set of server channels, $B(P_i)$, for each process P_i, can be done in constant time by making use of arrays *first* and *second* that were set up in the course of testing for triple-disjointedness (page 76). Once this set has been separated into server bundles for P_i, by local analysis, these may each be matched up with a preceding process in the network in the same manner. The act of checking each process for conformance to the protocol is again purely local to each process, and so $O(n)$. Hence, the overall complexity is $O(n)$.

Network Decomposition

Deadlock Checker implements the method for factorising deadlock analysis of Brookes and Roscoe (Theorem 6, page 34). This involves finding all the *disconnecting edges* of the network communication graph. Any such edge that is shown to be *conflict-free* may be removed. Deadlock analysis is then reduced to checking that each of the remaining network fragments (*essential components*) is deadlock-free. First, we need to construct the communication graph for the network and calculate its *vocabulary* Λ. This is straightforward given the alphabet of each process, which is calculated at the compilation stage.

Finding the disconnecting edges of the graph can be done in linear time, using a variant of the DFS algorithm. This is described in Appendix B. It is then required to check that the pair of processes (P, Q), which constitute each disconnecting edge, is conflict-free. This is done by checking that for every state σ of the subnetwork $\langle P, Q \rangle$, the following condition holds:

$$\neg(P \xrightarrow{\sigma, \Lambda} \bullet Q \wedge Q \xrightarrow{\sigma, \Lambda} \bullet P)$$

The specification checking technique described on page 76 is applied here. Any disconnecting edge that is found to be conflict-free is removed from the communication graph. When this phase is finished, the DFS algorithm is employed once again to assemble the residual components.

The subnetwork that each essential component represents is then assigned a name and placed on a 'stack' of networks. It may then be analysed by other methods. Deadlock Checker maintains a tree structure on this stack for hierarchical proofs. So, if and when deadlock freedom has been established for each essential component, the original network will be reported as being deadlock-free.

The following example demonstrates the construction of a hierarchical proof using Deadlock Checker. Consider the Telephoning, Arm-Wrestling, and Dining Philosophers. This is a system constructed from two tables of arm-wrestling philosophers, with a telephone link added between the two most senior philosophers. The CSP code is as follows:

```
PHILNAMES = {0,1,2,3,4}
FORKNAMES = {0,1,2,3,4}
TABLENAMES = {A,B}

pragma channel eats:TABLENAMES.PHILNAMES
pragma channel takes,drops:TABLENAMES.PHILNAMES.FORKNAMES
pragma channel wrestles:TABLENAMES.PHILNAMES.PHILNAMES
pragma channel phone

-- Junior philosopher: may challenge any of his seniors to an
-- arm-wrestling contest, between meals.He is left handed for
-- adherence to Resource Allocation Protocol.

JPHIL(x) = takes.x.0.4 -> takes.x.0.0 -> eats.x.0 ->
           drops.x.0.0 -> drops.x.0.4 -> JPHIL(x) |~|
           ( |~| j:{j | j <- PHILNAMES, 0<j} @ wrestles.x.0.j ->
           JPHIL(x) )

-- Intermediate philosopher: may challenge any of his seniors to
-- an arm-wrestling contest or accept a challenge from a junior,
-- between meals.

PHIL(i,x) = ( takes.x.i.i -> takes.x.i.((i-1)%5) -> eats.x.i ->
            drops.x.i.((i-1)%5) -> drops.x.i.i -> PHIL(i,x)   |~|
            ( |~| j:{j | j <- PHILNAMES, i<j} @ wrestles.x.i.j  ->
            PHIL(i,x) ) ) []
            ( [] j:{j | j <- PHILNAMES, j<i} @ wrestles.x.j.i  ->
            PHIL(i,x) )

-- Senior philosopher: accepts arm-wrestling challenges from his
-- juniors between meals; may also telephone senior philosopher
-- on other table or accept a call from him between meals.

SPHIL(x) = ( takes.x.4.4 -> takes.x.4.3 -> eats.x.4 ->
           drops.x.4.3 -> drops.x.4.4 -> SPHIL(x) ) []
           phone -> SPHIL(x) []
           ( [] j:{j | j <- PHILNAMES, j<4} @ wrestles.x.j.4 ->
           SPHIL(x) )

FORK(i,x) = takes.x.i.i -> drops.x.i.i -> FORK(i,x) []
            takes.x.((i+1)%5).i -> drops.x.((i+1)%5).i -> FORK(i,x)

--+ JPHIL(A),PHIL(1,A),PHIL(2,A),PHIL(3,A),SPHIL(A)
--+ JPHIL(B),PHIL(1,B),PHIL(2,B),PHIL(3,B),SPHIL(B)
--+ FORK(0,A),FORK(1,A),FORK(2,A),FORK(3,A),FORK(4,A)
--+ FORK(0,B),FORK(1,B),FORK(2,B),FORK(3,B),FORK(4,B)
```

The first stage of proving this network deadlock-free is to separate it into essential components (which in this case are the two tables of philosophers and forks).

```
Command (h for help, q to quit):l armphonephils.net
Command (h for help, q to quit):d
Network armphonephils.net is triple-disjoint
Network armphonephils.net is busy
SPHIL(A) and SPHIL(B) are conflict-free wrt vocab
```

```
Deadlock analysis reduced to:
<JPHIL(A), PHIL(1,A), PHIL(2,A), PHIL(3,A), SPHIL(A),
 FORK(0,A), FORK(1,A), FORK(2,A), FORK(3,A), FORK(4,A)>
<JPHIL(B), PHIL(1,B), PHIL(2,B), PHIL(3,B), SPHIL(B),
 FORK(0,B), FORK(1,B), FORK(2,B), FORK(3,B), FORK(4,B)>
```

The two new subnetworks have now been added to the stack. One of these is selected and then analysed first as a user resource network and then as a client-server network once its resources have been stripped away.

```
Command (h for help, q to quit):n (list networks)
armphonephils.net (unresolved)
armphonephils.net_0 (unresolved)     essential component
armphonephils.net_1 (unresolved)     essential component
Command (h for help, q to quit):s armphonephils.net_0
Command (h for help, q to quit):a
Network armphonephils.net_0 is busy
Network armphonephils.net_0 is triple-disjoint
Process FORK(4,A) acts as a resource
...
Process SPHIL(A) is not a resource
User process SPHIL(A) obeys resource allocation protocol
...
Deadlock analysis reduces to:
<JPHIL(A), PHIL(1,A), PHIL(2,A), PHIL(3,A), SPHIL(A)>

Command (h for help, q to quit):n
armphonephils.net (unresolved)
armphonephils.net_0 (unresolved)
armphonephils.net_1 (unresolved)
armphonephils.net_0_3 (unresolved)      resources stripped
Command (h for help, q to quit):c (display current network)
armphonephils.net_0_3
Command (h for help, q to quit):w
Network armphonephils.net_0_3 is busy
Network armphonephils.net_0_3 is triple-disjoint
Process JPHIL(A) obeys client-server protocol
clients(JPHIL(A)) =
{<wrestles.A.0.4>, <wrestles.A.0.3>,
 <wrestles.A.0.2>, <wrestles.A.0.1>}
servers(JPHIL(A)) = {}
...
Network armphonephils.net_0_3 is deadlock-free
Network armphonephils.net_0 is deadlock_free
```

To complete the deadlock analysis, the other essential component is analysed in the same manner

```
Command (h for help, q to quit):s armphonephils.net_1
Command (h for help, q to quit):a
...
Command (h for help, q to quit):w
...
Network armphonephils.net_1_4 is deadlock-free
Network armphonephils.net_1 is deadlock_free
Network armphonephils.net is deadlock_free
```

The proof of deadlock freedom for the network of Telephoning, Arm-wrestling, and Dining Philosophers has now been completed.

The algorithm for network decomposition requires the construction of the network communication graph and vocabulary. Using the following algorithm, it is possible to do this with complexity $O(n \log(n))$.

1. Start with the two arrays, *first* and *second*, that were constructed in order to establish triple disjointedness. Scan the two arrays to construct a list of pairs of the form $(first(e), second(e))$ such that both elements of the pair have been defined. This list will contain all the edges of the communication graph, but some of them may be duplicated. The set of values of e that contribute to this list is the vocabulary of the network.

2. Purge duplicate pairs from the list by performing a merge-sort (as described in [Paulson 1991]). This will result in a list of the edges in the communication graph.

The first step of this algorithm has complexity $O(n)$, where n is now taken as the number of edges in the communication graph; the second, which involves performing a merge-sort, has complexity $O(n \log(n))$.

To complete the network decomposition, local checks of process pairs remain to be done, which is $O(n)$, and also some global graph operations, which can also be done in $O(n)$ using the DFS. So, network decomposition can be done with overall complexity $O(n \log(n))$.

Restricting a Network to its Vocabulary

Deadlock Checker also has a feature to restrict a network to its vocabulary (only shared events are visible). By Lemma 5 (page 35), we know that if a network transformed in this way is deadlock-free, then so must have been the original network. This is useful, for instance, in the case of a network containing a cyclic-PO essential component, where some of the processes have had extra channels added for communication with processes in other essential components, which are not used according to the cyclic-PO paradigm.

However, it is possible for the act of hiding these extra channels to introduce divergence, which renders the resulting network unsuitable for deadlock analysis by our methods. This happens only when an arbitrarily long sequence of communications on the external channels is possible.

The technique that we use to restrict a network to its vocabulary comprises the following steps:

1. The vocabulary of the network Λ is calculated (those events that occur in the alphabet of two processes).
2. For each process P_i, all events in $\alpha P - \Lambda$ are hidden. In the normal form transition system for P, this involves relabelling with τ those transitions labelled with any of these events and removing acceptance sets that include these events.
3. The resulting transition system then needs to be renormalised. This is performed using Roscoe's algorithm, as described in Section 3.1.
4. The transformed network is placed on Deadlock Checker's network stack. If it is subsequently proven deadlock-free, then so must be the original network.

Checking for Livelock-Freedom

Deadlock Checker does not overlook the important property of livelock freedom. We implement the proof rule of Roscoe (Theorem 5, page 34), which works in many cases. The order in which the processes are supplied is significant here. The intention is to establish divergence freedom after all internal communications have been hidden. To do this, we need to show that no process can communicate indefinitely with those before it in the network list, as follows:

1. For each process P_i, we calculate the subset of its alphabet shared with predecessors in the process list and call this N_i.
2. We then consider the subgraph of the normal form transition system of P_i containing only those arcs labelled with events that lie in N_i.
3. If this subgraph contains no circuit, then P_i cannot communicate indefinitely with its predecessors in the network list.

3.4   TOWARDS A GENERAL PURPOSE ALGORITHM

The SDD algorithm

The tools described above are useful for proving deadlock freedom for networks constructed according to rigid design rules. But they do not allow for any improvisation by the creative programmer. The only scope for improvement is the addition of checking code for extra design rules, as and when required.

Despite these limitations, the design rules that are understood by Deadlock Checker enable the automatic proof of deadlock freedom for networks of an unprecedented size.

In this section, we shall describe the development of an alternative algorithm, which has no knowledge of design rules, and yet turns out to be able to do much of what the above tools offer, and more. A characteristic of deadlock states in busy, triple-disjoint networks is that they involve a cycle of ungranted requests (Theorem 1, page 31). So, if we can prove that a network can never have a cycle of ungranted requests, then it is deadlock-free. This is the fundamental principle that underlies the proof technique of variant functions (Theorem 2, page 31).

We now present a closely related alternative to variants: the *SDD* algorithm. This attempts to prove deadlock freedom by forming *a state dependence digraph*. This is basically a kind of giant wait-for digraph, where instead of having just a single vertex to represent a process, it has a different vertex for each minimal acceptance set of each normal form state.

1. Starting with a network of normalised transition systems $\langle P_1, P_2, \ldots, P_N \rangle$, we form the communication graph G and a digraph, SDD, which is initially empty.
2. For each edge (P, P') of G, we form the set $D(P, P')$ of all normal form state pairs (S, S') that process P and P' simultaneously.
3. For each pair (S, S') in each $D(P, P')$, for each minimal acceptance set A of S and for each minimal acceptance set A' of S', if P has an ungranted request to P', with respect to Λ – the vocabulary of the network, add $arc((P, S, A), (P', S', A'))$ to digraph SDD. And if P' has an ungranted request to P, with respect to Λ, add arc $((P', S', A'), (P, S, A))$.
4. We now have constructed a digraph, SDD. If this is circuit-free, the network is reported as being deadlock-free.

Theorem 10 *A busy, triple-disjoint network, which has a circuit-free state dependence digraph, is deadlock-free.*

Proof. Consider a busy, triple-disjoint network $V = \langle P_1, \ldots, P_n \rangle$. Suppose that V has a deadlock state

$$\sigma = (s, \langle X_1, \ldots, X_n \rangle)$$

In this state, there is a cycle of ungranted requests

$$P_{i_1} \xrightarrow{\sigma,\Lambda} \bullet P_{i_2} \xrightarrow{\sigma,\Lambda} \dots P_{i_k} \xrightarrow{\sigma,\Lambda} \bullet P_{i_1}$$

where each process P_{i_h} has performed trace $s \upharpoonright \alpha P_{i_h}$ and is refusing set X_{i_h}. Let this trace and refusal set correspond to state and acceptance set (S_{i_h}, A_{i_h}) of the normal form transition system for P_{i_h}. As P_{i_h} has an ungranted request to $P_{i_{h+1}}$ in state σ, the analysis of the two processes will produce an arc from vertex $(P_{i_h}, S_{i_h}, A_{i_h})$ to vertex $(P_{i_{h+1}}, S_{i_{h+1}}, A_{i_{h+1}})$ in the state dependence digraph. Performing this analysis of each pair of consecutive processes in the cycle of ungranted requests will result in a circuit in the state dependence digraph.

So we have shown that if there is a deadlock state of V, then there is a circuit in its state dependence digraph. This completes the proof□

Here is what happens when we apply the SDD algorithm to the Dining Philosophers network.

```
Command (h for help, q to quit):l phils.net
Command (h for help, q to quit):v
Network phils.net is triple-disjoint
Network phils.net is busy
Found possible cycle of ungranted requests:
FORK(0) ready to do drops.0.0 blocked by PHIL(0)
PHIL(0) ready to do takes.0.4 blocked by FORK(4)
FORK(4) ready to do drops.4.4 blocked by PHIL(4)
PHIL(4) ready to do takes.4.3 blocked by FORK(3)
FORK(3) ready to do drops.3.3 blocked by PHIL(3)
PHIL(3) ready to do takes.3.2 blocked by FORK(2)
FORK(2) ready to do drops.2.2 blocked by PHIL(2)
PHIL(2) ready to do takes.2.1 blocked by FORK(1)
FORK(1) ready to do drops.1.1 blocked by PHIL(1)
PHIL(1) ready to do takes.1.0 blocked by FORK(0)
```

The state dependence digraph for the Dining Philosophers is shown in Figure 3.9, constructed from the normal form transition systems shown in Figure 3.4. (As each process in the network is deterministic, there is exactly one minimal acceptance set corresponding to each state. In the case of a non-deterministic system, there would need to be more than one vertex to represent certain states in the state dependence digraph.) It contains a single circuit, representing the situation where each philosopher has picked up his left fork.

Figure 3.9: Construction of SDD for Dining Philosophers

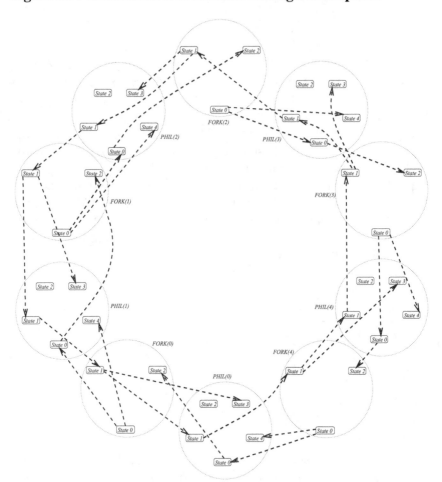

Although SDD works in many cases where variant functions could have been used, it is not quite so powerful, because an arbitrary number of maximal failures of a process can be mapped onto a single state in the normal form. One example of this is that the SDD technique will often fail for networks of cyclic processes that are amenable to the variant function technique. It will sometimes find a 'phantom' cycle of ungranted requests that cannot actually occur. For instance, consider what happens when we apply the algorithm to the deadlock-free toroidal cellular array.

```
Command (h for help, q to quit):l torus.net
Command (h for help, q to quit):v
Found possible cycle of ungranted requests:
CELL(2,3) ready to do e.2.3.right e.3.3.left
        blocked by CELL(3,3)
CELL(3,3) ready to do e.3.2.down e.3.3.up
        blocked by CELL(3,2)
```

```
CELL(3,2)  ready to do e.0.2.left e.3.2.right
           blocked by CELL(0,2)
CELL(0,2)  ready to do e.0.1.down e.0.2.up
           blocked by CELL(0,1)
CELL(0,1)  ready to do e.0.1.right e.1.1.left
           blocked by CELL(1,1)
CELL(1,1)  ready to do e.1.0.down e.1.1.up
           blocked by CELL(1,0)
CELL(1,0)  ready to do e.1.0.right e.2.0.left
           blocked by CELL(2,0)
CELL(2,0)  ready to do e.2.0.up e.2.3.down
           blocked by CELL(2,3)
```

The cycle of ungranted requests that has been reported cannot actually occur. Process CELL(2,3) can only have an ungranted request to CELL(3,3) if the latter has yet to complete its previous communication cycle. Also, no cyclic-PO process can ever have an ungranted request for another one that has completed more cycles. Following the potential cycle of ungranted requests in this way actually takes us back to the original process CELL(2,3) in the same state but on an earlier cycle. Clearly, a process cannot be on two *I/O* cycles simultaneously, so the potential cycle of ungranted requests is unreal. What it actually represents is a spiral of ungranted requests backwards in time.

We shall address this problem by refining the algorithm later on, but first let us explore the power of this prototype version in relation to some other design rules.

Applications of the SDD Algorithm
Theorem 11 *Any circuit-free client-server network composed of finite-state 'basic' processes has a circuit-free state dependence digraph.*

Proof. Consider a basic client-server network $V = \langle P_1, \dots, P_n \rangle$, with a circuit-free topology. This is deadlock-free by Rule 7 (page 52). We shall show that the state dependence digraph of V can never have a path of length 2, going through states of processes P_i, P_j, P_k, such that the relationship between P_i and P_j is client to server and the relationship between P_j and P_k is server to client. Then the circuit-freedom of the state dependence digraph will follow as a direct consequence of the circuit-freedom of the client-server digraph.

So first, suppose that there is an arc in the state dependence digraph

$$((P_j, S_j, A_j), (P_k, S_k, A_k))$$

where P_j communicates with P_k as server to client. This arc represents a potential ungranted request in the subnetwork

$$\langle P_j, P_k \rangle$$

and we can deduce, from the definition of the basic client-server protocol, that this can only occur when P_j is waiting for P_k to perform a *requisition* or *drip* event. It also follows from rule **(b)** that P_j is ready to perform all its server *requisition* and *drip* events, *i.e.*, they are all contained in A_j.

Now suppose that there is another arc in the state dependence digraph

$$((P_i, S_i, A_i), (P_j, S_j, A_j))$$

where P_i communicates with P_j as client to server. This arc represents an ungranted request in the subnetwork

$$\langle P_i, P_j \rangle$$

We already know that A_j contains every server *requisition* and *drip* event of P_j, so P_i must be waiting to communicate with P_j on a client *acknowledge* channel. But this is impossible by rule **(c)** of the protocol.

This contradiction means that there is no path in the state dependence digraph which goes from client to server and then from server to client. Therefore, as the client-server digraph is circuit-free, there can be no circuit in the state dependence digraph, so the network will be reported as being deadlock-free by the SDD algorithm. □

The SDD algorithm is clearly more powerful than the tool for checking deadlock freedom in basic client-server networks. It will always work and does not require the processes to be supplied in any particular order. However, as it has no intelligence regarding the actual protocol, it will probably be less useful as a debugging aid, especially for analysing networks constructed by teams rather than by individuals.

Theorem 12 *Any finite-state user-resource network that obeys the Resource Allocation Protocol has a circuit-free state dependence digraph.*

Proof. Consider a finite-state user-resource network that adheres to the Resource Allocation Protocol (page 61). Suppose that there is a circuit in its state dependence digraph. Due to the bipartite nature of the network, this circuit must run through a sequence of vertices of the form

$$\langle (U_{i_1}, S_{i_1}, A_{i_1}), (R_{j_1}, S_{j_1}, A_{j_1}), \ldots, (U_{i_k}, S_{i_k}. A_{i_k}), (R_{j_k}, S_{j_k}, A_{j_k}) \rangle$$

A user process can only have an ungranted request to a resource when it is waiting to claim it. We deduce that for each process R_{j_h}, state S_{j_h} is the normal form state where it is waiting to be released by the next process in the circuit, $U_{i_{h+1}}$ (addition modulo k), which is in state $S_{i_{h+1}}$ (see Figure 3.6).

Now the arc $((R_{j_h}, S_{j_h}, A_{j_h}), (U_{i_{h+1}}, S_{i_{h+1}}, A_{i_{h+1}}))$ represents an actual ungranted request within the subnetwork $\langle R_{i_h}, U_{i_{h+1}} \rangle$ so it must be possible for $U_{i_{h+1}}$ to be holding resource R_{j_h} in state $S_{i_{h+1}}$. As it also tries to claim resource $R_{j_{h+1}}$ from this state, it follows that $R_{j_h} > R_{j_{h+1}}$, by the terms of the protocol. Applying this result all the way around the circuit leads to the following contradiction:

$$R_{j_1} > R_{j_2} >, \ldots, R_{j_k} > R_{j_1} \quad \#$$

From this, we conclude that the state dependence digraph is actually circuit-free, and the network will be reported as being free of deadlock by the SDD algorithm□

In practice, the SDD algorithm also seems to be a useful tool for analysing user-resource networks, where the users communicate with each other, obeying the Extended Resource Allocation Protocol. It has no trouble in proving the Arm-Wrestling Dining Philosophers deadlock-free (or indeed the Telephoning Arm-Wrestling Dining Philosophers). It would be nice if whenever the subnetwork of user processes could be proven deadlock-free by the SDD algorithm so could be the whole network. However, this is not always the case, as the following example illustrates.

```
pragma channel a,b,c,c1,r1,c2,r2

U1 = (b -> U1 |~| a -> U1) [] c1 -> r1 -> U1
U2 = (c -> U2 |~| b -> U2) [] c2 -> r2 -> U2
U3 = a -> c -> U3
R = c1 -> r1 -> R [] c2 -> r2 -> R

--+ U1, U2, U3, R
```

Here, network $\langle U1, U2, U3 \rangle$ is provably deadlock-free by the SDD algorithm, but $\langle U1, U2, U3, R \rangle$ is not, even though it obeys the Extended Resource Allocation Protocol, and so is, in fact, deadlock-free. In the former case, events $c1, r1, c2$, and $r2$ lie outside the vocabulary, so there are no ungranted requests between $U1$ and $U2$ with respect to the vocabulary. But in the latter case the vocabulary includes all these events, and a potential cycle of ungranted requests is reported.

```
U2 ready to do b blocked by U1
U1 ready to do a blocked by U3
U3 ready to do c blocked by U2
```

Analysing Non-Standard Networks with SDD

Welch, Justo, and Willcock consider an interesting example of a client-server network where the basic protocol has been slightly abused [Welch *et al.* 1993]. The system comprises a *USER* process that is stimulated by regular 'ticks' from a *CLOCK* process. The *USER* process may reset the interval between ticks by means of a reset channel. Conceptually, process *USER* communicates as both a client and a server with process *CLOCK*. To avoid a circuit of client-server relationships, a 'circuit-breaker', consisting of a one-place overwriting buffer *OWB* together with a prompter *PROMPT*, is inserted along the reset channel. The client-server digraph of the resulting system is shown in Figure 3.10.

Figure 3.10: Client-Server Digraph for *CLOCK* Network

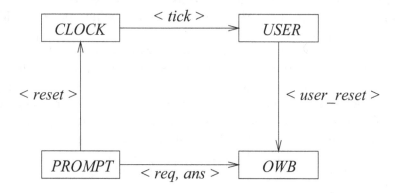

The machine-readable CSP code for this network is as follows:

```
pragma channel tock,user_reset,req,ans,reset,time_out

USER = tock -> (USER |~| user_reset -> USER)
PROMPT = req -> ans -> reset -> PROMPT
OWB = user_reset -> (req -> ans -> OWB [] OWB)
CLOCK = reset -> CLOCK [] time_out -> tock -> CLOCK

--+ PROMPT,CLOCK,USER,OWB
```

In this definition, *CLOCK* has an internal event *time_out*. This event represents a signal from an internal timer process that it is time to send out the next *tock*. Each process behaves according to the basic client-server protocol, apart from *OWB*. This process will shut down service on channel *req* whenever its buffer is empty. This contravenes rule **(b)** of the protocol. Nonetheless, Welch, Justo, and Willcock claim that the network is deadlock-free. This cannot be shown by the algorithm, which tests adherence to the basic client-server protocol, but it is no problem for the SDD algorithm.

```
Command (h for help, q to quit):l clock.net
Command (h for help, q to quit):v
Checking PROMPT with CLOCK
Checking PROMPT with OWB
Checking USER with CLOCK
Checking USER with OWB
Network clock.net is deadlock-free
```

This is a good example of a situation where a programmer's intuition has been automatically confirmed by SDD, avoiding the need for an analytic proof. As the system was designed with an aircraft control system in mind, this could be useful.

Accommodating Cyclic Processes

In general, the SDD is unable to prove networks of cyclic processes deadlock-free. However, these are important ingredients of many parallel algorithms. Fortunately, we can remedy the problem as follows. First of all, we extend the network analysis to produce a state dependence digraph with coloured arcs.

Remember that arc $((P, S, A), (P', S', A'))$ represents an ungranted request from process P in state S to process P' in state S'. If this can occur only when P and P' have each visited their initial state exactly the same number of times, we colour the arc *red*. Alternatively, if P must have visited its initial state more times than P', we colour the arc *green*. Otherwise, the arc is coloured *blue* to represent uncertainty.

The arc colouring is calculated in a similar way to the technique for specification checking described on page 77. First, we construct a set of records of the form

$$\langle \sigma_P, \sigma_{P'}, count \rangle$$

Each record contains a pair of states that P and P' may simultaneously be at together with a numeric label: *count*. This represents the number of times that the initial state of P has been 'crossed' minus the number of times that the initial state of P' has been crossed. A process is said to have crossed its initial state whenever it performs an event that returns it to its initial state. If the numeric labelling of state pairs is found to be inconsistent, *i.e.*, two records are found $\langle \sigma_P, \sigma_{P'}, count \rangle$ and $\langle \sigma_P, \sigma_{P'}, count' \rangle$ with $count \neq count'$, then *all* the numbering information regarding states of $\langle P, P' \rangle$ is discarded. Any ungranted request found between the two processes is regarded as 'uncertain' and coloured blue. If, however, a consistent numbering is discovered, it may be used to colour ungranted requests red, green, or blue in the manner described above.

To illustrate how the coloured state dependence digraph is constructed, let us return to the example of the two-place buffer from page 78. Recall that this was defined as follows:

$$LEFT = in \rightarrow mid \rightarrow LEFT$$
$$\alpha LEFT = \{in, mid\}$$

$$RIGHT = mid \rightarrow out \rightarrow RIGHT$$
$$\alpha RIGHT = \{mid, out\}$$

$$V = \langle LEFT, RIGHT \rangle$$

The exhaustive search for records of the form $(\sigma_{LEFT}, \sigma_{RIGHT}, count)$ proceeds as follows. First, we have

$$pending = \{(0, 0, 0)\}, done = \{\}$$

Check $(0,0,0)$; possible transition is in; neither initial state is crossed; leads to record: $(1,0,0)$. Now we have

$$pending = \{(1,0,0)\}, done = \{(0,0,0)\}$$

Check $(1,0,0)$; possible transition is mid; initial state of $LEFT$ is crossed; leads to record: $(0,1,1)$. Now we have

$$pending = \{(0,1,1)\}, done = \{(0,0,0), (1,0,0)\}$$

Check $(0,1,1)$; possible transitions are in and out; if in is performed, neither initial state is crossed, but if out is performed, initial state of $RIGHT$ is crossed; lead to records $(1,1,1)$ and $(0,0,0)$. Now we have

$$pending = \{(1,1,1)\}, done = \{(0,0,0), (1,0,0), (0,1,1)\}$$

Check $(1,1,1)$; possible transition is out; initial state of $RIGHT$ is crossed; leads to record $(1,0,0)$. Now we have

$$pending = \{\}, done = \{(0,0,0), (1,0,0), (0,1,1), (1,1,1)\}$$

Now we have discovered all the state pairs in which processes $LEFT$ and $RIGHT$ may simultaneously rest. For each pair, we have found an invariant property count that represents the number of times that $LEFT$ has visited its initial state more than $RIGHT$.

Suppose that *LEFT* and *RIGHT* are embedded in some network V', which has a vocabulary Λ containing events *in* and *out*. We find that state pair $(0,0)$ involves an ungranted request from *RIGHT* to *LEFT* with respect to Λ. This is represented as a red arc in the coloured state dependence digraph because the value of *count* is always zero for this state pair. We also find that state pair $(1,1)$ involves an ungranted request from *LEFT* to *RIGHT* with respect to Λ. This is represented as a green arc in the coloured state dependence digraph because the value of *count* is always 1 for this state pair. The other state pairs $(0,1)$ and $(1,0)$ do not involve any ungranted requests.

So the analysis of *LEFT* and *RIGHT* would result in the addition of the following arcs to the coloured state dependence digraph for V':

$$\text{Red arc}: \left(\left(\begin{array}{ll} Process: & RIGHT \\ State: & 0 \\ Acceptance\ set: & \{mid\} \end{array}\right), \left(\begin{array}{ll} Process: & LEFT \\ State: & 0 \\ Acceptance\ set: & \{in\} \end{array}\right)\right)$$

$$\text{Green arc}: \left(\left(\begin{array}{ll} Process: & LEFT \\ State: & 1 \\ Acceptance\ set: & \{mid\} \end{array}\right), \left(\begin{array}{ll} Process: & RIGHT \\ State: & 1 \\ Acceptance\ set: & \{out\} \end{array}\right)\right)$$

When the same analysis is applied to processes *FORK(0)* and *PHIL(0)* in the Dining Philosophers network, inconsistencies are found in the *count* variable. This is obvious by the fact that process *FORK(0)* may cross its initial state any number of times by cycling on events *takes.1.0* and *drops.1.0* before process *FORK(0)* has performed any event at all. In this case, all the ungranted requests detected between the processes would appear as blue arcs in the coloured state dependence digraph.

Any circuit in the *coloured* state dependence digraph containing a blue arc remains a potential cause of deadlock, so does any circuit that contains only red arcs. But a circuit containing no blue arcs and at least one green arc does not represent a cycle of ungranted requests in the network, for the ungranted requests cannot all occur simultaneously.

We check for deadlock freedom as follows. First, we use a variant of the DFS to remove all those arcs from the digraph that do not lie on any circuit (described in Appendix B). If any blue arc remains, then there is potential for deadlock. Otherwise, all the remaining arcs must be red or green. The only risk of deadlock in this case is if there is a circuit consisting only of red arcs, so we remove all the green arcs and then see whether any circuit still remains.

Given that the motivation for the CSDD algorithm was to be able to handle cyclic processes, the following result is not altogether surprising.

Theorem 13 *Take a deadlock-free network of cyclic-LOP processes. Its coloured state dependence digraph contains neither a blue arc nor a circuit of red arcs.*

Proof. Let $V = \langle P_1, \ldots, P_n \rangle$ be a deadlock-free network of cyclic-LOP processes. Each process is finite-state by definition. We observe that although a cyclic-LOP process does not necessarily visit the same states on each cycle, its initial state is always crossed between cycles. Between any two visits to a particular state, such a process performs every event in its alphabet the same number of times, equal to the number of times that it has crossed its initial state.

Consider a subnetwork of two communicating cyclic-LOP processes, $\langle P_i, P_j \rangle$. Suppose that these processes may simultaneously be in states σ_{P_i} and σ_{P_j}. Between two particular visits to this state pair, suppose that P_i performs m_i cycles of events in αP_i and P_j performs m_j cycles of events in αP_j. As the processes communicate with each other, we have

$$\alpha P_i \cap \alpha P_j \neq \{\}$$

Let c be an event from $\alpha P_i \cap \alpha P_j$. Between the two visits to the state pair, event c has been performed m_i times by P_i and has also been performed m_j times by P_j. So, $m_i = m_j$; in other words, P_i and P_j must each cross their initial state the same number of times between any two visits to a given pair of states.

This means that when the subnetwork $\langle P_i, P_j \rangle$ is analysed for records of the form

$$(\sigma_{P_i}, \sigma_{P_j}, count)$$

where *count* represents the number of times more that P_i has crossed its initial state than P_j, we shall find that *count* is invariant for any pair of states.

A cyclic-LOP process can only have an ungranted request to another process that has performed the same number of cycles or one less cycle. It follows that the coloured state dependence digraph for V contains only red and green arcs and no blue arcs. Suppose that a circuit of red arcs was found. This would correspond to a sequence of processes

$$\langle P_{i_1}, \ldots, P_{i_k}, P_{i_l} \rangle$$

such that each process P_{i_h} would have a state where it could perform some event c_h with its successor in the sequence but not be able to perform some other event c_{h-1} with its predecessor in the sequence, despite having completed the same number of cycles. This would imply the existence of a circuit in the $\triangleright$ relation,

$$c_1 \triangleright \ldots \triangleright c_k \triangleright c_1$$

which would contradict Theorem 8 (page 45), so there can be no circuit of red arcs in the coloured state dependence digraph for V. It follows that V will be passed as deadlock-free by the CSDD algorithm□

Unlike the SDD algorithm, the CSDD algorithm has no problem with the toroidal cellular array.

```
Command (h for help, q to quit):x
Network torus.net is deadlock-free
```

Although the new algorithm can handle cyclic-LOP networks, it is not guaranteed to be able to prove deadlock freedom for cyclic-PO networks in general, as these may have legitimate cycles of ungranted requests at times, despite being deadlock-free.

Note that when it is required to use CSDD to prove deadlock freedom for hybrid networks, including cyclic subnetworks, one has to be careful that the extra communications added to the cyclic processes do not remove the property that they should each cross their initial state exactly once after each cycle.

Each stage in the analysis has $O(n)$ complexity (where n is the number of edges in the communication graph), given our usual assumptions about the number of states and events of each process, except for the construction of the communication graph and vocabulary, which we have shown to be feasible with $O(nlog(n))$ complexity. Thus, the CSDD algorithm can be performed with complexity $O(nlog(n))$.

Allowing for Weak Conflict

Another useful way to extend the SDD algorithm is to incorporate Theorem 3 (page 33). Recall that if a network is shown to be free of strong conflict, then any deadlock state must contain a cycle of ungranted requests of length at least three. This means that if the state dependence digraph of a strong conflict-free network contains no circuits of length three or more, then the network is deadlock-free regardless of how many circuits of length two are found.

The property of strong conflict freedom may be checked during the construction of the state dependence digraph at virtually no extra cost. If a strong conflict is found, it is reported, and the algorithm terminates.

Searching for circuits of length three or more in a simple digraph may be performed by the following algorithm. For each arc (v, v') of the digraph $D(V,A)$, use the DFS to look for a path from v' to v in the digraph $D(V, A - ((v', v)))$. If no such path is found, then the digraph has no circuit of length three or more.

For our coloured digraph, we adapt this algorithm as follows. First, we check that there is no circuit of length at least three containing a blue arc. For each blue arc (v, v'), we use the DFS to look for a path from v' to v in the digraph $D(V, A - ((v', v)))$. If no such circuit is found, then we remove all the blue and green arcs from the digraph and search for a circuit of length three or more in the resulting red digraph. If none is found, we have proved deadlock freedom.

In the prototype version of Deadlock Checker, this improvement has been included as part of the CSDD test but not the SDD test. Unfortunately, the technique that we use to check for circuits of length three or more increases the complexity to $O(n^2)$, as a DFS search may now be required for each arc in the digraph. However, there may well exist a more efficient technique than this.

Potential for Further Improvement

Despite the improvements that we have made to the original SDD algorithm, the possibility remains of detecting bogus cycles of ungranted requests. One way in which this has been observed in practice has been the detection of a circuit in the state dependence digraph that crosses more than one state of the same process. It is clearly impossible for a process to be in two states at the same time, so such a circuit cannot represent a *real* cycle of ungranted requests.

Suppose that we now colour the *vertices* of the state dependence digraph, where each colour represents the states of a particular process. To avoid the problem described above, we are looking for an algorithm to determine whether this digraph contains a circuit in which every vertex has a different colour. At the time of writing, no efficient algorithm has been found to decide this question in general (which may easily be shown to belong to class NP). However, even an inefficient algorithm would be useful in the case where the state dependence digraph contains only a small number of circuits.

A more promising approach involving this vertex colouring is based on the concept of *request selector functions* [Dathi 1990, Roscoe 1995]. Suppose that there is some vertex of the state dependence digraph, $v = (P, S, A)$, which has outgoing arcs to vertices that have several different colours. Now suppose that we choose one particular such colour $C(v)$ and delete every outgoing arc from v that points to a vertex with a different colour from $C(v)$. If the stripped-down version of the state dependence digraph that results contains no circuit, then it is still the case that the network must be deadlock-free. The result still holds no matter how many vertices v are treated in this manner.

This may be informally justified as follows. What we have actually done is to choose a particular process to which P has a request when it is accepting the events of A in state S, and to ignore requests to other processes. For any deadlock state of the network, we could still find a cycle of ungranted requests corresponding to a circuit in the stripped-down state dependence digraph.

It is thought that this technique should be useful as follows. Suppose that a state dependence digraph has been constructed and is found to contain circuits. An algorithm is envisaged that would attempt to find a sequence of vertex and colour selections leading to the removal of sufficient arcs to render the digraph circuit-free and hence prove deadlock freedom.

We could also extend the power of the checker to embrace the design rule of Brookes and Roscoe (Theorem 4, page 33). We might do this by adding an extra dimension to the coloured state dependence digraph: arcs would either be 'flashing' or 'non-flashing'. An ungranted request from a state of process P to a state of process Q would be set to be flashing only if it had been shown that Q must have communicated with P more recently than with any other process in that situation. Then any circuit of flashing arcs, of length greater than two, could not represent a real cycle of ungranted requests in the network, as the ungranted requests could not occur simultaneously. This follows from the reasoning we used to prove Theorem 4.

It would also be relatively straightforward to allow for networks where processes can terminate. Dathi defines a network as *prudent* if no process ever tries to communicate with one that is only willing to perform an event $\sqrt{}$ [Dathi 1990]. With a slight adjustment to the definition of deadlock freedom to allow for termination, the CSDD algorithm could be implemented in exactly the same way for a network containing terminating processes, which had been shown to be prudent.

Due to the exponential state explosion as a network grows in size, it seems unlikely that there is an algorithm for deciding deadlock freedom for finite-state processes that is both efficient and *complete*. There are certain networks for which deadlock freedom depends on some crucial property of global states. For instance, the analysis of a 'token-ring' system in [Brookes and Roscoe 1991] involves proving that there is exactly one 'token' present in any state of the system. The techniques described above, being based on local analysis, would be inadequate for this particular task. However, there is certainly much scope for automatic assistance in performing analyses of this nature. The limitations of proving deadlock freedom purely by local analysis are further discussed in [Roscoe 1995].

There is clearly potential for expanding the armoury of efficient verification techniques such as CSDD. If these are to be used in anything other than a trial-and-error manner, they must be backed up with further design rules that will enable networks to be built not only deadlock-free but that may be easily verified.

4

ENGINEERING APPLICATIONS

INTRODUCTION

This chapter is intended to illustrate how the preceding work may be applied to real problems in software engineering. The occam programming language is introduced for this purpose, and its relationship with CSP is elaborated. We then present three examples of designing and building industrial-scale deadlock-free concurrent systems.

The first problem considered is the numerical solution to Laplace's equation using the method of *successive over-relaxation*. This is typical of the sort of computationally intensive task that parallel computers are often required to perform. Deadlock freedom is incorporated into the design by using the cyclic-PO paradigm.

Next, we describe the construction of a deadlock-free message routing program for a multiprocessor computer system. Traditionally, one of the most laborious tasks in parallel programming has been the routing of messages between processes that run on non-adjacent physical processors. For this reason, a great deal of effort has been directed towards developing deadlock-free message routing programs. The intention of this is to separate all the physical messages passing onto a lower conceptual level and to implement *virtual* channels between any two locations in a processor network. Here, we describe the construction of a *store and forward* deadlock-free message routing system for a network of eight processors configured as a cube. The client-server paradigm is used for this purpose. We then modify the program to implement *wormhole* routing, which is generally more efficient than store and forward routing. In doing so, we breach the rules of the client-server paradigm. However, the resulting system is proven deadlock-free using the SDD algorithm.

The final example involves a published algorithm for a control system for a television studio. The system is shown to be prone to deadlock. However, with a simple modification, it may be transformed into a circuit-free client-server network resulting in guaranteed deadlock freedom.

Table 4.1 – Relationship between occam and CSP

occam	CSP

SEQ
  P
  Q
	$P; Q$

PAR
  P
  Q
	$(P\|[\alpha P\|\alpha Q]\|Q)\backslash(\alpha P \cap \alpha Q)$

a?x	$a?x \rightarrow SKIP$
b!y	$b!y \rightarrow SKIP$

ALT
  c?x
    P
  d?y
    Q
	$c?x \rightarrow P \Box d?y \rightarrow Q$

IF
  b
    P
  NOT b
    Q
	$P \triangleleft b \triangleright Q$

WHILE TRUE P	$\mu X \bullet P; X$

4.1 THE OCCAM PROGRAMMING LANGUAGE

The occam programming language, which is described in [INMOS 1988], was originally derived from the CSP model. The notation is somewhat different, but it is elegant nonetheless. The language is unusual in that the indentation of the lines of code is syntactically significant. In the absence of an efficient compiler for CSP itself, occam represents the most appropriate implementation language for programs designed using CSP specifications.

Table 4.1 lists some roughly equivalent constructions between the two languages. One significant difference is that the occam parallel operator incorporates automatic hiding of communication events, which remain visible in CSP. This feature has the potential to introduce the phenomenon of livelock into a network. There are also certain extra-high-level aspects to occam, such as prioritised external choice, timers, and the assignment of variables.

Ideally, we would like to build checks for deadlock freedom and livelock freedom into occam compilers. One way to do this would be to convert into CSP state-transition digraphs as used by the algorithms of Deadlock Checker. The translation of occam into CSP is considered informally in [Scattergood and Seidel 1994]. Problems arise from the treatment of the values of variables, leading to a potential explosion in the state size of the resulting CSP. For instance, a process that has a local variable that can take any real numeric value usually needs to have at least one CSP state for each value.

Realistically, we have to look at how much information can be discarded in the conversion without removing any potential deadlocks or livelocks so that they may be detected. We need to establish a safe level of abstraction that maximises the performance of the tools. It is usually safe to represent communication events in occam purely by their channel names in the CSP specification. The one exception is when using a *variant protocol* on a particular channel. If the inputting process is unwilling to accept the type of datum offered by the outputting process, a local deadlock will ensue. (However, if an exhaustive case list is offered by the inputting process, there can be no problem, but this may be impractical.)

The opposite route of translation from CSP to occam is considered in [Scott 1994]. The conversion is based on denotational semantics for occam [Goldsmith *et al* 1993].

4.2   CASE STUDIES

Numerical Solution to Laplace's Equation

We consider the design and implementation of a parallel program to calculate the first-order finite difference solution of Laplace's equation by the method of *successive over-relaxation*. This technique is described in [Fox *et al* 1988].

The two-dimensional Laplace equation is given by

$$\frac{\partial^2 U}{\partial x^2} + \frac{\partial^2 U}{\partial y^2} = 0$$

We seek a solution for the unknown potential, U, across a rectangular grid domain, given fixed boundary values. We define an $m \times n$ array $U^{(k)}$ to represent the kth approximation to the result. Individual array elements are denoted $U_{ij}^{(k)}$, where i ranges from 0 to $m - 1$ and j ranges from 0 to $n - 1$. Each generation of U is calculated by the following iterative equation (we assume that $U^{(0)}$ is known):

$$U_{ij}^{(k)} = \frac{\omega}{4}[U_{i-1,j}^{(k)} + U_{i,j-1}^{(k)} + U_{i+1,j}^{(k-1)} + U_{i,j+1}^{(k-1)}] + (1 - \omega)U_{ij}^{(k-1)}$$

$$\text{where } (0 < i < m - 1) \wedge (0 < j < n - 1)$$

$$U_{ij}^{(k)} = U_{ij}^{(0)} \quad \text{otherwise (fixed boundary condition)}$$

where ω is the *relaxation factor*.

The design of this parallel program is similar to the toroidal cellular automaton in Section 2.1. We allocate a cyclic-PO process, $CELL(i,j)$, to each grid element, connected by input and output channels to its neighbours. Process $CELL(i,j)$ is responsible for calculating successive iterations of $U_{i,j}$. (The processes representing the boundary elements perform a trivial task as their state is fixed.) Each process also has bidirectional client-server connections to a control process, *CONTROL*, for periodic resets.

It will be seen that the iterative equation imposes an ordering on channels between neighbouring grid cells – on a given *I/O* cycle, a process needs to wait for its immediate left and upper neighbours to compute their new states before it can inquire about their new values and compute its own new state. Figure 4.1 illustrates a feasible deadlock-free channel ordering for this strategy. Based on this labelled connection diagram, the communication pattern of each process in the network is defined as follows:

$$CHAT(i,j) = SKIP \sqcap out.i.j \rightarrow in.i.j \rightarrow SKIP$$
$$CELL(i,j) = CHAT(i,j);$$

$$\left(\begin{array}{l} (e.i.j.left \rightarrow SKIP) \quad ||| \\ (e.i.j.up \rightarrow SKIP) \end{array} \right);$$

$$\left(\begin{array}{l} (e.(i+1) \cdot j \cdot left \rightarrow SKIP) \quad ||| \\ (e.i \cdot (j+1) \cdot up \rightarrow SKIP) \quad ||| \\ (e.(i-1) \cdot j \cdot right \rightarrow SKIP) \quad ||| \\ (e.i.(j-1) \cdot down \rightarrow SKIP) \end{array} \right);$$

$$\left(\begin{array}{l} (e.i.j.right \rightarrow SKIP) \; ||| \\ (e.i.j.down \rightarrow SKIP) \end{array} \right);$$

$$CELL(i,j)$$

where $(0 < i < m - 1) \wedge (0 < j < n - 1)$

$$CELL(0,j) = CHAT(0,j);$$
$$e.1.j.left \rightarrow e.0.j.right \rightarrow CELL(0,j)$$

$$CELL(m-1,j) = CHAT(m-1,j);$$
$$e.(m-1).j.left \rightarrow e.(m-2).j.right \rightarrow CELL(m-1,j)$$

where $(0 < j < n - 1)$

$$CELL(i,0) = CHAT(i,0);$$
$$e.i.1.up \rightarrow e.i.0.down \rightarrow CELL(i,0)$$

$$CELL(i,n-1) = CHAT(i,n-1);$$
$$e.i.(n-1).up \rightarrow e.i.(n-2).down \rightarrow CELL(i,n-1)$$

where $(0 < i < m - 1)$

$$CONTROL = (\square_{i=1}^{m-2} \square_{j=1}^{n-2} out.i.j \rightarrow in.i.j \rightarrow CONTROL) \; \square$$

$$\left(\square_{i=1}^{m-2} \left(\begin{array}{l} out.i.0 \rightarrow in.i.0 \rightarrow CONTROL \; \square \\ out.i.(n-1) \rightarrow in.i.(n-1) \rightarrow CONTROL \end{array} \right) \right) \square$$

$$\left(\square_{j=1}^{n-2} \left(\begin{array}{l} out.0.j \rightarrow in.0.j \rightarrow CONTROL \; \square \\ out.(m-1).j \rightarrow in.(m-1).j \rightarrow CONTROL \end{array} \right) \right)$$

Figure 4.1: Labelled Connection Diagram for Laplace Solver

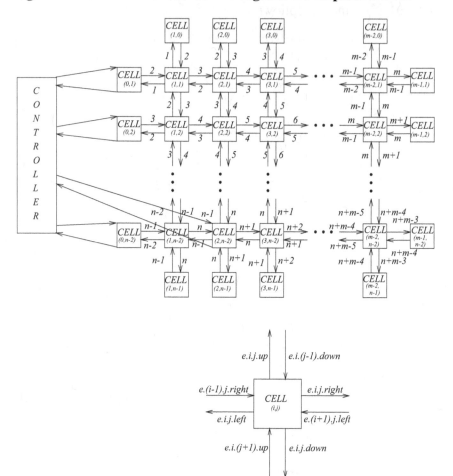

The CSDD algorithm of Deadlock Checker can be used to verify that this particular network is deadlock-free for given values of n and m. It is straightforward to develop an occam implementation of the program based on this specification. There follows a possible implementation of an interior cell process.

```
PROC CELL (VAL INT i, j)
  REAL32 w, x, y, z, state:
  INT k, ncycles:
  SEQ
    state := 0.0 (REAL32)
    WHILE TRUE
      SEQ
        out[i][j] ! state              -- Communicate with
        in[i][j] ? state; ncycles      -- CONTROL
        k := 0
        WHILE k<ncycles
          SEQ                          -- Perform next
            k:=k+1                     -- iteration
            PAR
                e[i][j][LEFT] ! state
                e[i][j][UP] ! state
            PAR
                e[i+1][j][LEFT] ? w
                e[i][j+1][UP] ? x
                e[i-1][j][RIGHT] ? y
                e[i][j-1][DOWN] ? z
            state := (((((w+x)+y)+z) *
                    (OMEGA/4.0(REAL32))) +
                    (state *(1.0(REAL32) - OMEGA)))
            PAR
                e[i][j][RIGHT] ! state
                e[i][j][DOWN] ! state
  :
```

A Message Router

Suppose we wished to realise the Laplace solving network on a parallel machine constructed from a collection of Inmos transputers. We would most probably need to run a considerable number of *CELL* processes on each processor. However, each transputer only has four hardware links to neighbouring processors, which would be insufficient compared with the number of communication channels that would need to be implemented. Some form of multiplexing would be required.

Historically, this has been a somewhat irritating problem for programmers of parallel machines. Even for a simple process network, a large amount of work has often been needed to map it onto the target hardware configuration. Frequently, the resulting implementation has not even been semantically equivalent to the original, sometimes resulting in unforeseen deadlocks.

Using a deadlock-free routing algorithm, it is possible to implement unlimited virtual channels between transputers that *are* semantically equivalent to synchronous hardware links [Roscoe 1988b]. This work can be performed by a compiler, either partially or totally, freeing the programmer from much low-level effort.

We now consider the design of a deadlock-free routing algorithm for a network of eight transputers configured as a cube, based on a program from [Shumway 1990]. The client-server paradigm will be employed. The guiding principle that we shall use is to assign a *level* to each link between processors, and then to ensure that any message arriving at a processor on level n can only depart on a level greater than n. In this way, deadlock can be avoided by ensuring that all messages travel 'upwards' to their destination, which guarantees that the client-server digraph is circuit-free. Figure 4.2 illustrates the router process topology superimposed on top of the processor topology. Each processor runs a separate process to control each of its input and output links. It also runs two interface processes, *TO* and *FROM*. The former collects messages that have arrived at their destination and passes them on to the local application process. The latter routes messages from the local application destined for other processes.

Links in the x direction are assigned level one, those in the y direction level two, and those in the z direction level three. To send a message to its destination, the strategy used is first to get the x coordinate right, then the y coordinate, and finally the z coordinate.

The abstract CSP design of the program is listed below:

```
coords = {0,1}
direction = {dx, dy, dz}
change_direction = {xy,xz,yz}

-- 3 input links for each transputer

pragma channel i : coords.coords.coords.direction

-- Internal channels

pragma channel in, out : coords.coords.coords.direction
pragma channel q: coords.coords.coords.change_direction

-- Channels for interface to applications program

pragma channel to, from : coords.coords.coords

-- Processes to service input links

INX(x,y,z) = i.x.y.z.dx -> (out.x.y.z.dx -> INX(x,y,z)  |~|
                            q.x.y.z.xy -> INX(x,y,z) |~|
                            q.x.y.z.xz -> INX(x,y,z))

INY(x,y,z) = i.x.y.z.dy -> (out.x.y.z.dy -> INY(x,y,z)   |~|
                            q.x.y.z.yz -> INY(x,y,z))

INZ(x,y,z) = i.x.y.z.dz -> out x.y.z.dz -> INZ(x,y,z)

-- Processes to service output links

OUTX(x,y,z) = in.x.y.z.dx -> i.((x+1)%2).y.z.dx -> OUTX(x,y,z)

OUTY(x,y,z) = in.x.y.z.dy -> i.x.((y+1)%2).z.dy -> OUTY(x,y,z)    []
              q.x.y.z.xy -> i.x.((y+1)%2).z.dy -> OUTY(x,y,z)

OUTZ(x,y,z) = in.x.y.z.dz -> i.x.y.((z+1)%2).dz -> OUTZ(x,y,z)    []
              q.x.y.z.xz -> i.x.y.((z+1)%2).dz -> OUTZ(x,y,z)     []
              q.x.y.z.yz -> i.x.y.((z+1)%2).dz -> OUTZ(x,y,z)

-- Interface to application program
```

```
TO(x,y,z) =    out.x.y.z.dx -> to.x.y.z -> TO(x,y,z)   []
               out.x.y.z.dy -> to.x.y.z -> TO(x,y,z)   []
               out.x.y.z.dz -> to.x.y.z -> TO(x,y,z)

FROM(x,y,z) = from.x.y.z -> (    in.x.y.z.dx -> FROM(x,y,z)  |~|
                                 in.x.y.z.dy -> FROM(x,y,z)  |~|
                                 in.x.y.z.dz -> FROM(x,y,z)  )

-- Now specify network for Deadlock Checker. The processes are
-- listed according to their "client-server" ordering.

--+FROM(0,0,0),FROM(0,0,1),FROM(0,1,0),FROM(0,1,1),
--+FROM(1,0,0),FROM(1,0,1),FROM(1,1,0),FROM(1,1,1),
--+OUTX(0,0,0),OUTX(0,0,1),OUTX(0,1,0),OUTX(0,1,1),
--+OUTX(1,0,0),OUTX(1,0,1),OUTX(1,1,0),OUTX(1,1,1),
--+INX (0,0,0),INX (0,0,1),INX (0,1,0),INX (0,1,1),
--+INX (1,0,0),INX (1,0,1),INX (1,1,0),INX (1,1,1),
--+OUTY(0,0,0),OUTY(0,0,1),OUTY(0,1,0),OUTY(0,1,1),
--+OUTY(1,0,0),OUTY(1,0,1),OUTY(1,1,0),OUTY(1,1,1),
--+INY (0,0,0),INY (0,0,1),INY (0,1,0),INY (0,1,1),
--+INY (1,0,0),INY (1,0,1),INY (1,1,0),INY (1,1,1),
--+OUTZ(0,0,0),OUTZ(0,0,1),OUTZ(0,1,0),OUTZ(0,1,1),
--+OUTZ(1,0,0),OUTZ(1,0,1),OUTZ(1,1,0),OUTZ(1,1,1),
--+INZ (0,0,0),INZ (0,0,1),INZ (0,1,0),INZ (0,1,1),
--+INZ (1,0,0),INZ (1,0,1),INZ (1,1,0),INZ (1,1,1),
--+TO  (0,0,0),TO  (0,0,1),TO  (0,1,0),TO  (0,1,1),
--+TO  (1,0,0),TO  (1,0,1),TO  (1,1,0),TO  (1,1,1)
```

Figure 4.2: Cube Router

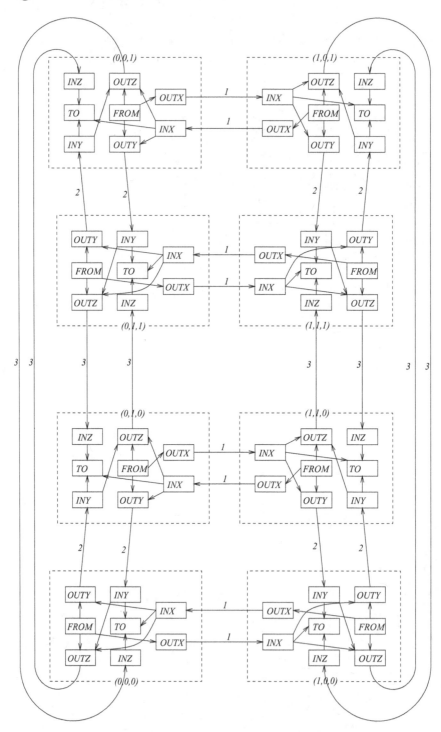

This initial design avoids the issue of how to make routing decisions. When a message arrives on an input channel at a particular process, it is redirected non-deterministically along any one of its output channels. Despite this disregard for any routing information, the design is sufficiently robust to be proven deadlock-free by adherence to the client-server protocol. In this case, each individual channel is a client-server bundle of size one. A process acts as a server on its input channels and as a client on its output channels. This means that the client-server digraph for the system is the same as the connection digraph. The condition that messages must always travel upwards guarantees that they are circuit-free. (Note that the network could be represented rather more compactly using an exploded client-server digraph, treating the set of processes that run on each transputer as a single composite client-server process.) Deadlock freedom is easily verified using Deadlock Checker.

```
Welcome to Deadlock Checker
Command (h for help, q to quit):l router.net
Command (h for help, q to quit):w
Network router.net is busy
Network router.net is triple-disjoint
Process FROM(0,0,0) obeys client-server protocol
clients(FROM(0,0,0)) =
{<in.0.0.0.dz>,
 <in.0.0.0.dy>,
 <in.0.0.0.dx>}
servers(FROM(0,0,0)) =
{}
...
Process TO(1,1,1) obeys client-server protocol
clients(TO(1,1,1)) =
{}
servers(TO(1,1,1)) =
{<out.1.1.1.dx>,
 <out.1.1.1.dy>,
 <out.1.1.1.dz>}
Network router.net is deadlock-free
```

The system may also be shown to be livelock-free at this stage.

```
Command (h for help, q to quit):t
Network router.net is triple-disjoint
Network router.net is livelock-free
```

It is interesting to note that each of the sixty-four processes of this network may, or may not, be holding a message at any given time, which means that the system as a whole has at least 2^{64} states. This would put it well out of the range of any program using exhaustive state checking.

From the abstract design, we are now able to develop a working occam implementation without difficulty. For instance, here is the process INX, which runs on each transputer.

```
PROC INX(VAL INT x, y, z, processor)
  ... local declarations
```

```
WHILE TRUE
  SEQ
    i[x][y][z][dx] ? length :: packet
    IF
      packet[0] = processor -- Arrived at destination
        out[x][y][z][dx] ! length :: packet
      ycoord(packet[0]) <> y -- Need to fix Y coordinate
        q[x][y][z][xy] ! length :: packet
      TRUE                   -- Need to fix Z coordinate
        q[x][y][z][xz] ! length :: packet
:
```

The technique of assigning levels to processor links in order to effect a routing strategy can be generalised to processor networks of arbitrary construction. (Details are given in [Debbage *et al* 1993] and [Pritchard 1992].) For certain topologies, it is necessary to multiplex a number of virtual links on different levels, along a particular hardware link, in order to guarantee that there is always an upward path between each pair of processors. Figure 4.3 illustrates link-labelling schemes for a ring and a grid. The former involves the use of virtual multiplexed links, but the latter does not. Multiplexing is a potential pitfall and must be implemented with great care. A good method of multiplexing is described in [Jones and Goldsmith 1988]. A process is constructed that utilises a single transputer link and yet is semantically equivalent to a collection of independent one-place buffers. (Note that it cannot be assumed in general that it is safe to add buffering along a channel of a network. Any such modification needs to be considered as part of the overall deadlock analysis.)

Figure 4.3: Routing Strategies for Ring and Grid

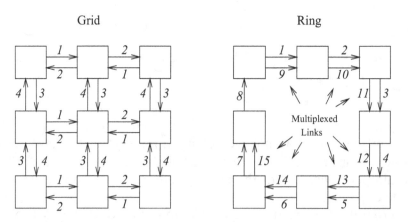

Wormhole Routing
Wormhole routing differs from store and forward routing in that a message is split up into small packets, and these are sent across the network

together by cutting a virtual path through it and holding this path open until the last packet has passed through. The following CSP code illustrates a modification to the design of the cube router that uses this strategy:

```
coords = {0,1}
direction = {dx, dy, dz}
change_direction = {xy,xz,yz}
packets = {data, end}

-- 3 input links for each transputer

pragma channel i : coords.coords.coords.direction.packets

-- Internal channels

pragma channel in, out : coords.coords.coords.direction.packets
pragma channel q: coords.coords.coords.change_direction.packets

-- Channels for interface to applications program

pragma channel to, from : coords.coords.coords.packets

-- Processes to service input links

INX(x,y,z) = i.x.y.z.dx.data ->
                (out.x.y.z.dx.data -> INX1 (x,y,z)   |~|
                 q.x.y.z.xy.data -> INX2 (x,y,z,xy)  |~|
                 q.x.y.z.xz.data -> INX2 (x,y,z,xz))
INX1(x,y,z) = i.x.y.z.dx?p -> out.x.y.z.dx.p ->
                if p == data then INX1 (x,y,z) else INX(x,y,z)
INX2(x,y,z,cd) = i.x.y.z.dx?p -> q.x.y.z.cd.p ->
                if p == data then INX2 (x,y,z,cd) else INX(x,y,z)
INY(x,y,z) = i.x.y.z.dy.data ->
                (out.x.y.z.dy.data -> INY1 (x,y,z)   |~|
                 q.x.y.z.yz.data -> INY2 (x,y,z,yz) )
INY1(x,y,z) = i.x.y.z.dy?p -> out.x.y.z.dy.p ->
                if p == data then INY1 (x,y,z) else INY(x,y,z)
INY2(x,y,z,cd) = i.x.y.z.dy?p -> q.x.y.z.cd.p ->
                if p == data then INY2 (x,y,z,cd) else INY(x,y,z)

INZ(x,y,z) = i.x.y.z.dz.data ->
                out.x.y.z.dz.data -> INZ1(x,y,z)
INZ1(x,y,z) = i.x.y.z.dz?p -> out.x.y.z.dz.p ->
                if p == data then INZ1(x,y,z) else INZ(x,y,z)

-- Processes to service output links


OUTX(x,y,z) = in.x.y.z.dx.data ->
                i.((x+1)%2).y.z.dx.data -> OUTX1(x,y,z)
OUTX1(x,y,z) = in.x.y.z.dx?p -> i.((x+1)%2).y.z.dx.p ->
                if p == data then OUTX1 (x,y,z) else OUTX(x,y,z)

OUTY(x,y,z) = in.x.y.z.dy.data ->
                i.x.((y+1)%2).z.dy.data -> OUTY1(x,y,z) []
                q.x.y.z.xy.data ->
                i.x.((y+1)%2).z.dy.data -> OUTY2(x,y,z,xy)
OUTY1(x,y,z) = in.x.y.z.dy?p -> i.x.((y+1)%2).z.dy.p ->
                if p == data then OUTY1 (x,y,z) else OUTY(x,y,z)
OUTY2(x,y,z,cd) = q.x.y.z.cd?p -> i.x.((y+1)%2).z.dy.p ->
                if p == data then OUTY2(x,y,z,cd) else OUTY(x,y,z)

OUTZ(x,y,z) = in.x.y.z.dz.data ->
```

```
                 i.x.y.((z+1)%2).dz.data -> OUTZ1(x,y,z)   []
                 q.x.y.z.xz.data ->
                 i.x.y.((z+1)%2).dz.data -> OUTZ2(x,y,z,xz) []
                 q.x.y.z.yz.data ->
                 i.x.y.((z+1)%2).dz.data -> OUTZ2(x,y,z,yz)
OUTZ1(x,y,z) = in.x.y.z.dz?p -> i.x.y.((z+1)%2).dz.p ->
                 if p == data then OUTZ1(x,y,z) else OUTZ(x,y,z)
OUTZ2(x,y,z,cd) = q.x.y.z.cd?p -> i.x.y.((z+1)%2).dz.p ->
                 if p == data then OUTZ2(x,y,z,cd) else OUTZ(x,y,z)

-- Interface to application program

TO(x,y,z) = out.x.y.z?d?p -> to.x.y.z.p -> TO(x,y,z)

FROM(x,y,z) = from.x.y.z.data ->
                 (in.x.y.z.dx.data -> FROM2(x,y,z,dx)  |~|
                  in.x.y.z.dy.data -> FROM2(x,y,z,dy)  |~|
                  in.x.y.z.dz.data -> FROM2(x,y,z,dz)  )
FROM2(x,y,z,d) = from.x.y.z?p -> in.x.y.z.d.p ->
                 if p == data then FROM2(x,y,z,d) else FROM(x,y,z)
```

This design actually contravenes the rules for client-server communication. Once the first packet of a message has been received, a process will then only be prepared to communicate on one of its server channels. However, the network is still easily proven deadlock-free using the SDD algorithm. Livelock-freedom is also preserved.

```
Command (h for help, q to quit):l wormhole.net
Command (h for help, q to quit):v
Network wormhole.net is triple-disjoint
Network wormhole.net is busy
Checking INZ(1,1,1) with TO(1,1,1)
Checking INZ(1,1,0) with TO(1,1,0)
...
Network wormhole.net is deadlock-free
Command (h for help, q to quit):t
Network wormhole.net is triple-disjoint
Network wormhole.net is livelock-free
```

This is an interesting example because, although a reasonable solution was achieved to the initial problem using only design rules, in order to develop a more efficient solution, it was necessary to bend the rules.

A Television Studio Control System

This example differs from the previous two, in that we start with a published algorithm that is closely related to our design rules but ultimately breaches them. First, we show that this algorithm is theoretically prone to deadlock. Then, we consider how the design can be modified to remove this problem. The system considered is, in many ways, a very fine piece of engineering. The fact that it has such a fundamental flaw is by no means a reflection on its developers. The main motivation for this thesis is that such problems are almost inevitable in practice unless suitable design rules for avoiding them are provided.

The algorithm was developed by N. Miller and Y. Bouchlaghem for the control of audio communications in a television studio [Miller and Bouchlaghem 1995]. The system, which is called 'Commander', consists of up to 384 control panels, each of which has an associated analogue audio sound channel. The control panels are each connected to one of four central racks via a 96-way multiplexor. Each of these racks is then connected to a cross-bar switch, which is used to control audio connections between users. The four racks are also connected to each other so as to pass on switching requests from users and to request information.

The hardware is based on transputers. There is one behind each control panel, and there are three in each rack: one to manage the multiplexor, one to control the cross-bar switch, and the third responsible for communication with the other racks and the implementation of the high-level system functionality. Figure 4.4 shows the connection digraph for the processes running on this system. Apart from the inter-rack connections, all message passing conforms to the client-server paradigm. Each control panel runs a process *PANEL*, which is a client of a multiplexor control process *PANEL.MGR*. This in turn is a client of a rack management process *RACK.MGR*, which is a client of a process *XBAR.MGR* that controls a cross-bar switch.

The only place where Miller and Bouchlaghem diverge from the client-server paradigm is in inter-rack communications. Unfortunately, we shall see that their system can deadlock because of this. We shall concentrate on the CSP definition for the subnetwork of *RACK.MGR* processes. (Note that this definition conceals communications with *XBAR-MGR* processes.)

$$RACK.MGR(i) = from.panel.mgr.i \rightarrow (ACTION(i); RACK.MGR(i)) \square$$
$$(\square_{j \neq i} chan.j.i.req \rightarrow chan.i.j.ack \rightarrow RACK.MGR(i))$$

$$ACTION(i) = SKIP \sqcap (\sqcap_{j \neq i} INITIATE(i, j, req))$$

$$INITIATE(i,j,x) = \left(\begin{array}{l} chan.i.j!x \rightarrow \square_{k \neq i} chan.k.i?z \rightarrow \\ (SKIP \lhd (z = ack) \rhd INITIATE(i,k,ack)) \\ \square_{k \neq i} chan.k.i?z \rightarrow chan.i.j!x \rightarrow \\ (SKIP \lhd (z = ack) \rhd INITIATE(i,k,ack)) \end{array} \right) \square$$

$$RACKS = \left| \begin{array}{ll} RACK.MGR(0), & RACK.MGR(1), \\ RACK.MGR(2), & RACK.MGR(3) \end{array} \right|$$

Each rack manager process is initially waiting either for a signal to arrive from its panel manager or a request from another rack. If it receives a request from another rack, this is immediately answered. If it receives a signal from its panel manager, it may need to communicate with another rack. In this case, it goes into 'action' mode. First, it sends out its request and, in parallel, waits for a message to arrive from another rack. This message could either be the required answer to its request or another request requiring an answer. In the former case, the process returns to its initial state; in the latter, it begins another cycle of parallel input and output. This time, the output is an answer to the request that has just been received. The process continues with cycles of parallel inputs and outputs until an answer has been received to its original request.

When network *RACKS* is analysed by Deadlock Checker using the SDD algorithm, it is reported that strong conflict can occur between neighbouring processes. As the number of states of the system is relatively small (about three thousand), exhaustive state analysis is feasible using the FDR tool. This reveals that the network may deadlock after the following trace:

$$\left\langle \begin{array}{ccc} from.panel.mgr.0, & from.panel.mgr.1, & from.panel.mgr.2, \\ from.panel.mgr.3, & chan.2.3.req & chan.0.1.req \end{array} \right\rangle$$

Figure 4.4: Connection Digraph for COMMANDER

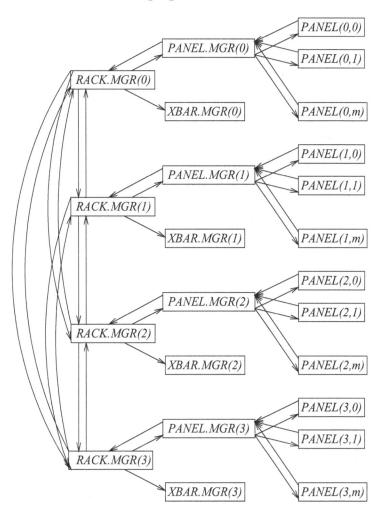

At this point, both *RACK.MGR(0)* and *RACK.MGR(2)* are waiting for a message to arrive from another rack. But it is possible that *RACK.MGR(1)* and *RACK.MGR(3)* have both already committed to sending a message to each other, which would mean deadlock. Of course, we have only considered a subnetwork of the system as a whole, so we need to check that this deadlock could still arise in the wider context. It is fairly obvious that this is indeed the case.

Miller and Bouchlaghem report that their software has been running without problems on a system with over one hundred users for some time. Perhaps this indicates that there is a very low probability of deadlock occurring. However, this type of uncertainty could certainly not be tolerated in a safety-critical application, such as an air traffic control system.

It is a simple matter to modify the definition of *RACK.MGR* to render the system deadlock-free through adherence to the client-server protocol. This is achieved by splitting the process into two levels, *RACK.MGR'* and *RACK.MGR"*. Each lower-level process *RACK. MGR'* handles signals from the local panel manager as a server and also makes requests to any of the four higher-level processes *RACK. MGR"* as a client. The new CSP definitions are as follows:

$$RACK.MGR'(i) = from.panel.mgr.i \to \sqcap_{j=0}^{3} req.i.j \to ack.i.j \to RACK.MGR'(i)$$

$$RACK.MGR''(i) = \square_{j=0}^{3} req.j.i \to ack.j.i \to RACK.MGR''(i)$$

$$RACKS' = \left(\begin{array}{ll} RACK.MGR'(0), & RACK.MGR'(1), \\ RACK.MGR'(2), & RACK.MGR'(3), \\ RACK.MGR''(0), & RACK.MGR''(1), \\ RACK.MGR''(2), & RACK.MGR''(3) \end{array} \right)$$

The client-server digraph of this improved design is given in Figure 4.5. It is circuit-free, which guarantees deadlock freedom for the new system. It is notable that, as well as being deadlock-free, the new design is far simpler and somewhat more elegant. This shows how, far from being overly restrictive, design rules can enhance the creative process of parallel software design.

Figure 4.5: Client-Server Digraph for Improved Design

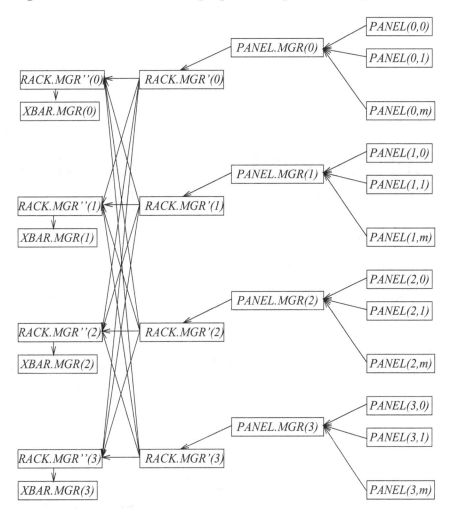

CONCLUSIONS AND DIRECTIONS FOR FUTURE WORK

Due to problems like deadlock and livelock, parallel programs are significantly more difficult to design than serial ones. Perhaps for this reason, concurrent programming has been slow to take off. Our hunger for computing power is largely being satisfied by the continual development of ever-faster serial processors. However, there are limits to serial hardware technology that are likely to be approached within the next twenty years. Explicit parallelism will then become the only means of extending the performance of computers, and the field of concurrent programming will finally have come of age.

This thesis has described a collection of simple design rules for constructing large-scale parallel systems that can never deadlock. We have also detailed efficient techniques for the machine verification of adherence to these rules. More interestingly, a technique for efficiently proving deadlock freedom was discovered that, despite having no intelligence regarding the design rules, was found to be capable of proving deadlock freedom for networks constructed according to the majority of them. However, it is important to note that this algorithm, which is called CSDD, is far from a complete proof technique for deadlock freedom. There are many deadlock-free networks, which it cannot prove to be so. It works by checking a stronger property than deadlock freedom – one that can be established in $O(n^2)$ time complexity for networks of finite-state processes, being based purely on local analysis. This compares favourably with the exponential complexity of using FDR for deadlock analysis. On the other hand, the FDR approach is complete for finite-state networks.

The CSDD algorithm is sufficiently simple that it seems suitable for

The Design and Construction of Deadlock-Free Concurrent Systems

inclusion in compilers for high-level parallel languages such as occam. However, to make this feasible, we need to look at methods to restrict the size of the state spaces to be analysed.

A tool to verify the validity of an *abstraction*, or indeed, to perform abstraction automatically, would be very useful. Recall that abstraction is the act of replacing detailed communication events with their channel names in CSP networks. In effect, this means 'throwing away the data'. This technique has been used throughout the thesis to simplify CSP expressions to be analysed for deadlock freedom. In this way, infinite-state networks may be proven deadlock-free by the analysis of finite-state abstractions. A formal statement of the property is given in [Roscoe 1995].

Without the use of abstraction, the operational representation of even a very simple occam process might be vast. A technique for conversion from occam to CSP is described in [Scattergood and Seidel 1994] that addresses this problem.

The deadlock analysis techniques that we have described are based on a static network of non-terminating processes grouped together by a single level of parallelism. We rely on each process having a relatively small number of states. Efficient deadlock analysis is then possible because we avoid constructing the state transition system for the network as a whole. However, if there were a large degree of embedded parallelism in any component process of the network, we would still need to analyse some unwieldy operational representations.

A good illustration of this problem is a program from [Jones and Goldsmith 1988], which implements Conway's Game of Life using an array of *I/O-PAR* processes, each with 16 channels. The fact is that the abstract operational form of each of these harmless-looking processes has 65536 states. This would certainly make the pairwise process checking performed by the CSDD algorithm impractical.

It should be possible to develop transformational techniques to cope with networks like this, which remove all the embedded parallelism to the outer layer. For instance, consider the *I/O-SEQ* process

$$P = (a \rightarrow SKIP \parallel b \rightarrow SKIP); (c \rightarrow SKIP \parallel d \rightarrow SKIP); P$$

We transform this process into a subnetwork of five purely sequential processes as follows:

$$P' = s_1 \rightarrow s_2 \rightarrow f_1 \rightarrow f_2 \rightarrow s_3 \rightarrow s_4 \rightarrow f_3 \rightarrow f_4 \rightarrow P'$$
$$Q_1 = s_1 \rightarrow a \rightarrow SKIP; f_1 \rightarrow Q_1$$
$$Q_2 = s_2 \rightarrow b \rightarrow SKIP; f_2 \rightarrow Q_2$$
$$Q_3 = s_3 \rightarrow c \rightarrow SKIP; f_3 \rightarrow Q_3$$
$$Q_4 = s_4 \rightarrow d \rightarrow SKIP; f_4 \rightarrow Q_4$$

Events s_i and f_i are 'start' and 'finish' commands for each subprocess Q_i, sent out by the master process P'. The following equivalence may be shown (using FDR):

$$P = PAR(\langle P', Q_1, Q_2, Q_3, Q_4 \rangle) \backslash \{s_i, f_i | i = 1,2,3,4\}$$

We could use this as follows. First, we could prove divergence freedom for P by using Deadlock Checker to prove livelock freedom for

$$PAR(\langle P', Q_1, Q_2, Q_3, Q_4 \rangle)$$

This would allow us to substitute $\{P', Q_1, Q_2, Q_3, Q_4\}$ for P into any network to be tested for deadlock freedom.

Similarly, transforming an *I/O-PAR* process with 16 channels, such as in the Jones and Goldsmith program, would result in a subnetwork with seventeen processes, each one being a purely sequential cyclic process with just a handful of states. This would provide a representation suitable for analysis by Deadlock Checker.

It would be very useful to explore general situations where such transformations might be applied. This approach ought to be particularly applicable to occam programs, where it is common to have several layers of embedded parallelism.

Deadlock freedom is only the tip of the iceberg when it comes to proving the desirable properties of concurrent systems. If we were to design a signalling system for trains based on these methods, it would certainly be a good idea to prove the system deadlock-free, but it would be somewhat more important to ensure that no two trains could ever collide. The FDR tool can be used to do proofs like this by exhaustive state analysis. However, due to the exponential state explosion as a network grows in size, this method cannot be used for very large networks. Certainly, not the Great Western Railway network.

Specifications that prohibit undesirable actions are known as *safety conditions* and are generally expressed purely in terms of traces, refusal sets being irrelevant. One approach to proving the safety properties of large systems is to factorise the proofs into smaller manageable parts. To prove that no two trains can ever collide, we might attempt to prove separately a large number of statements of the form: "*TRAINA* and *TRAINB* will never collide on the track section governed by *SIGNAL1*". If we could show that this statement held true for the subnetwork

$$\langle TRAINA, TRAINB, SIGNAL1 \rangle$$

then clearly it would hold for the network as a whole. This could be done using the refinement checker FDR as the number of states in the subnetwork ought to be manageable. There is scope for developing a logical inference tool to assist with proofs of this kind.

It is also common to write specifications that insist that some desirable form of behaviour should occur. For instance, we might specify that the electric doors of a train's carriages should never refuse to be opened when the train is standing on a platform. Specifications such as this are called *liveness conditions*, and they require the full expressive power of the failures model.

Dathi's thesis [Dathi 1990] contains the attractive idea of transforming a general failures specification problem into a proof of deadlock freedom. Given a concurrent system $V = \langle P_1, \ldots, P_n \rangle$ and a specification S, we want to show the refinement relation

$$failures(S) \supseteq failures(PAR(V) \backslash (\alpha V - \alpha S))$$

Dathi defines a process transformation function δ so that proving the refinement reduces to showing that the network

$$\langle \delta(S), P_1, \ldots, P_n \rangle$$

is deadlock-free. Basically, $\delta(S)$ is a 'testing' process that guarantees to deadlock the network whenever $PAR(V) \backslash (\alpha V - \alpha S)$ exhibits any behaviour that is illegal for S. Unfortunately, the process $\delta(S)$ is not itself deadlock-free, so we cannot use any of the local analysis techniques described in this thesis to prove the refinement. However, Dathi defines a similar transformation function δ^* that produces better-behaved processes $\delta^*(S)$. In this case, it is first necessary to prove, by other means, that

$$traces(S) \supseteq traces(PAR(V) \backslash (\alpha V - \alpha S))$$

We may then show that the failures specification is satisfied by proving the network
$$\langle \delta^*(S), P_1, \ldots, P_n \rangle$$
to be deadlock-free. It should be straightforward to automate this technique for inclusion in a tool like Deadlock Checker. Design rules might then be formulated for the type of specifications that could be checked.

A different approach is likely to be required when dealing with issues relating to the correctness of computation rather than communication. Recalling the program to solve Laplace's equation in Chapter 4, we have proven that this program cannot deadlock, but we are yet to show that it accurately calculates a solution to the problem. The prototype CSP code does not contain enough information to do this.

We need to consider the refinement in the final occam version. For this program, any conventional operational representation would be vast. To construct it, we would effectively have to perform the entire computation for every single possible variety of initial conditions. Ideally, what is required is a two-tiered form of operational semantics so that information regarding computation is represented on a separate level from information regarding communication.

Another important issue that has not been considered in this thesis is time. A major motivation for parallel computation is the speed of results. Therefore, we are likely to have hard real-time requirements for the systems that we design. If an airman presses the button to switch off the autopilot, he should not have to wait for half an hour for anything to happen. The state of the art regarding the use of timed CSP is described in [Davies 1993]. A complete method for proving adherence to timed specifications is presented, but the author recognises that the large number of proofs required for applications of a significant size is likely to be infeasible. Therefore, it would seem that there is a need for design rules to be discovered that would facilitate the development of real-time systems. Perhaps the most promising of the design rules considered here, from this point of view, is the cyclic paradigm. The processes could be synchronised to operate with a computation phase and a communication phase of fixed time, say δt. The time for various external operations to be effective should then be easy to predict as a multiple of δt. This idea is similar to the BSP paradigm of L. Valiant (documented in [Oxford Parallel 1995]).

A VISION FOR THE FUTURE

Apparently, there is still some work to be done before the construction of large-scale parallel programs can be regarded as a thoroughly safe engineering discipline.

Hopefully, this thesis has outlined an approach to one of the major problems that is clearly practical. Ease of use and simplicity of presentation are major goals in developing tools for engineers.

In the near future, there is an exciting prospect of an integrated CSP development environment, as illustrated in Figure 4.6. Programs can be systematically refined from their abstract specifications using a number of tools to perform functions such as refinement checking, abstraction checking, real-time specification checking, conversion to and from high-level programming languages, and, of course, deadlock and livelock analysis. In the event of a potential deadlock being detected, the tool would be able to point back to the exact position of the source of each process involved.

CSP is a most elegant language, and it would be nice if it could be used directly for actual programming rather than having to convert to another language such as occam. Then, we could use the same notation all the way through, from specification to implementation. To make an efficient CSP compiler, one would need to enforce certain restrictions, such as the restriction in occam that external choice can only be applied to input channels. There would also need to be some thought applied to the treatment of the state of variables and their scope. Probably the language that we would finally arrive at would be functionally very similar to occam, but it would look like CSP. Of course, some people might not consider CSP notation to provide the most *readable* presentation style for concurrent software, preferring the use of words rather than symbols. There is no reason why a verbose isomorphism of CSP should not be provided for such people, rather than a different language.

By making life easier for engineers, we might reduce the potential for software-precipitated catastrophes. However, it is very important that we always maintain a clear view of the limitations of formal methods. For instance, they cannot guard against a leaky specification that fails to incorporate vital safety information. There will always be a human decision-making aspect to software construction. By making the programming environment helpful, intuitive, and secure, we can help ensure that the right decisions are made.

Figure 4.6: CSP Toolkit – A Vision for the Future

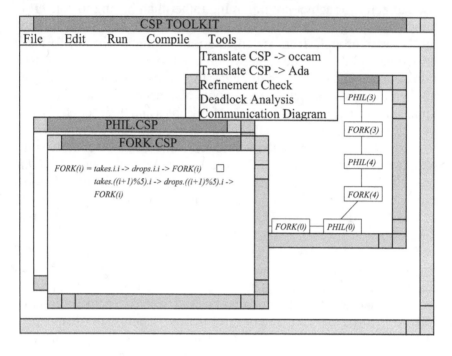

REFERENCES

[Brinch Hansen 1973] P. Brinch Hansen. *Operating System Principles*, Prentice-Hall, 1973.

[Brookes 1983] S. D. Brookes. *A Model for Communicating Sequential Processes,* Oxford University D.Phil. Thesis, 1983.

[Brookes and Roscoe 1985a] S. D. Brookes and A. W. Roscoe. *An Improved Failures Model for Communicating Processes*, Springer LNCS 197, 1985.

[Brookes and Roscoe 1985b] S. D. Brookes and A. W. Roscoe. *Deadlock Analysis in Networks of Communicating Processes*, Logic and Models of Concurrent Systems NATO ASI series F. Vol 13. Springer, 1985.

[Brookes and Roscoe 1991] S. D. Brookes and A. W. Roscoe. *Deadlock Analysis in Networks of Communicating Processes*, Distributed Computing (1991)4, Springer-Verlag.

[Chandy and Misra 1979] K. M. Chandy and J. Misra. *Deadlock Absence Proofs for Networks of Communicating Processes*, Information Processing Letters, Volume 9, number 4,1979.

[Dathi 1990] N. Dathi. *Deadlock and Deadlock-Freedom*, Oxford University D.Phil. Thesis, 1990.

[Davies 1993] J. Davies. *Specification and Proof in Real Time CSP*, Cambridge University Press, 1993.

[Debbage *et al* 1993] M. Debbage, M. B. Hill, and D. A. Nicole. *Global Communications on Locally Connected Message-Passing Parallel Computers*, Concurrency, Practice and Experience, September 1993.

[Dewdney 1989] A. K. Dewdney. *A Cellular Universe of Debris, Droplets, Defects and Demons*, Scientific American, August 1989.

[Dijkstra 1965] E. W. Dijkstra. *Cooperating Sequential Processes*, Technological University Eindhoven, The Netherlands, 1965. (Reprinted in *Programming Languages*, F. Genuys, ed., Academic Press, New York, 1968.)

[Dijkstra 1982] E. W. Dijkstra. *A Class of Simple Communication Patterns*, Selected Writings on Computing: A Personal Perspective, Springer-Verlag, 1982.

[Even 1979] S. Even, *Graph Algorithms*, Computer Science Press, Inc., 1979.

[Formal Systems 1993] *FDR User Manual and Tutorial*, Formal Systems (Europe) Ltd. 3 Alfred Street, Oxford OX1 4EH, 1993.

[Fox *et al* 1988] G. Fox, et al. *Solving Problems on Concurrent Processors*, Prentice Hall, 1988.

[Goldsmith *et al* 1993] M. Goldsmith, A. W. Roscoe, and B. G. O. Scott. *Denotational Semantics for* occam2 Transputer Communications, Volume 1 Number 2, 1993 and Volume 2 Number 1, 1994, Wiley.

[Hoare 1985] C. A. R. Hoare. *Communicating Sequential Processes*, Prentice-Hall, 1985.

[INMOS 1988] INMOS Limited. occam2 *Reference Manual*, Prentice Hall, 1988.

[Jones and Goldsmith 1988] G. Jones and M. Goldsmith. *Programming in occam2*, Prentice-Hall, 1988.

[Knapp 1987] E. Knapp. *Deadlock Detection in Distributed Databases*, ACM Computing Surveys, Vol 19, No 4, December 1987.

[Macfarlane 1992] D. Macfarlane. *A Practical Investigation of Parallel Genetic Algorithms and their Application to the Structuring of Artificial Neural Networks*, University of Buckingham D.Phil. Thesis, 1992.

[Mairson 1989] H. Mairson. *On Axiomatic Characterizations of CSP* (Unpublished), Department of Computer Science, Brandeis University, Waltham, Massachusetts 02254, 1989.

[Marcino 1995] P. Marcino. *Re:deadlock avoidance/recovery*, Contribution to newsgroup comp.databases.sybase, 12th September 1995.

[Martin 1995] J. M. R. Martin. *Deadlock Checker User Guide and Technical Manual*, University of Buckingham Internal Report (Department of Mathematics, Statistics and Computer Science), 1995.

[Martin *et al* 1994] J. M. R. Martin, I. East, and S. Jassim. *Design Rules for DeadlockFreedom*, Transputer Communications, September 1994.

[Martin and Welch 1996] J. M. R. Martin and P. H. Welch. *A Design Strategy for Deadlock-Free Concurrent Systems*, in preparation.

[Miller and Bouchlaghem 1995] N. Miller and Y. Bouchlaghem. *A Reliable Studio Control System – The Theory and the Practice*, Transputer Applications and Systems '95, IOS Press, 1995.

[Oxford Parallel 1995] *The BSP Model*, Oxford Parallel, available via *WWW* as `http://www.comlab.ox.ac.uk/oucl/oxpara/bspmodel.htm`.

[Paulson 1991] L. Paulson. *ML for the Working Programmer*, Cambridge University Press, 1991.

[Pritchard 1992] D. J. Pritchard. *Load Balanced Deadlock-Free Deterministic Routing of Arbitrary Networks*, Proceedings of the 1992 ACM Computer Science Conference, 1992.

[Roscoe 1988a] A. W. Roscoe. *Unbounded Non-determinism in CSP*, Oxford University Computing Laboratory (Technical Monograph PRG-67), 1988.

[Roscoe 1988b] A. W. Roscoe. *Routing Messages Through Networks: An Exercise in Deadlock Avoidance*, Proceedings of the 7th occam User Group Technical Meeting, IOS Press, 1988.

[Roscoe 1994] A. W. Roscoe. *Model Checking* CSP A Classical Mind, Prentice-Hall, 1994.

[Roscoe 1995] A. W. Roscoe. *Notes on CSP*, Oxford University Lecture Notes, 1995.

[Roscoe and Dathi 1986] A. W. Roscoe and Naiem Dathi. *The Pursuit of Deadlock Freedom*, Oxford University Computing Laboratory (Technical Monograph PRG-57), 1986.

[Scattergood 1992] B. Scattergood. *A Parser for CSP*, available by anonymous ftp from `ftp.comlab.ox.ac.uk`, 1992.

[Scattergood and Seidel 1994] B. Scattergood and K. Seidel. *Converting occam to CSP*, Transputer Applications and Systems '94, IOS Press, 1994.

[Scott 1994] B. G. O. Scott. *Translating Timed CSP Processes to* occam2, Transputer Applications and Systems '94, IOS Press, 1994.

[Shumway 1990] M. Shumway. *Deadlock-Free Packet Networks*, INMOS Central Applications Group, Colorado Springs, 1990.

[Welch 1987] P. H. Welch. *Emulating Digital Logic Using Transputer Networks*, Parallel Architectures and Languages Europe, LNCS 258, Springer-Verlag, 1987.

[Welch *et al* 1993] P. H. Welch, G. R. R. Justo, and C. J. Willcock. *High-Level Paradigms for Deadlock-Free High-Performance Systems*, Transputer Applications and Systems '93, IOS Press, 1993.

[Wilson 1985] R. J. Wilson. *Introduction To Graph Theory (Third Edition)*, Longman Scientific & Technical, 1985.

[Wolfson 1987] O.Wolfson. *The Overhead of Locking (and Commit) Protocols in Distributed Databases*, ACM Transactions on Database Systems, Vol. 12, No. 3, September 1987.

Appendix A
PARTIAL ORDERS

A *partial order* is a relation $\leq$ acting on a set S, which satisfies

$$(x \leq y) \wedge (y \leq z) \implies x \leq z$$

$$(x \leq y) \wedge (y \leq x) \iff x = y$$

The following are examples of partial orders:

(A) The set of subsets of the natural numbers, ordered by inclusion ($\subseteq$), *e.g.*,

$$\{1,2,3,4\} \subseteq \{1,2,3,4,5\}$$

(B) The finite sequences of letters ordered lexicographically, *i.e.*, as a dictionary, where the first letter is most significant, *e.g.*,

$$\langle\rangle \leq \langle a \rangle \leq \langle aa \rangle \leq \langle b \rangle \leq \langle bazzz \rangle$$

An *upper bound* of a subset A of S is an element z of S, such that

$$\forall x \, : \, A.x \leq z$$

A *least upper bound* of a subset A of S, written as $\sqcup A$, is an upper bound of A, such that, for any upper bound x of A, $\sqcup A \leq x$.

In example A, above, consider the subset $S = \{\{1,2\}, \{2,3\}, \{3,1\}\}$. The least upper bound for S is $\{1,2,3\}$.

A *directed set* is a nonempty subset $\Delta \subseteq S$, such that

$$\forall x, y : \Delta. \quad \exists z : \Delta. \quad (x \leq z) \wedge (y \leq z)$$

A partial order S is said to be *complete* if it has a least element $\bot$, and every directed set $\Delta \in S$ has a least upper bound.

Example B, above, is not a complete partial order. Consider the subset

$$U = \{\langle a \rangle, \langle aa \rangle, \langle aaa \rangle, ...\}$$

U is clearly directed, yet it has no least upper bound.

Example A, however, is a complete partial order. Any subset is directed and has a least upper bound. There is a least element – the empty set.

If S and T are two complete partial orders and $f : S \rightarrow T$, then f is said to be *monotonic* if

$$\{x, y\} \subseteq S \wedge x \leq y \Longrightarrow f(x) \leq f(y)$$

Also f is *continuous* if whenever $\Delta \subseteq S$ is directed, $\sqcup\{f(x)|x \in \Delta\}$ exists and equals $f(\sqcup\Delta)$.

Lemma 7 *Suppose S, T are complete partial orders and $f : S \rightarrow T$ is continuous. Then, f is monotonic.*

Theorem 14 (Tarski) *If S is a complete partial order, and $f : S \rightarrow S$ is continuous, then f has a least fixed point (i.e., $\exists x : S$, such that $f(x) = x$ and, if $f(y) = y$, then $x \leq y$). This is given by*

$$\sqcup\{F^n(\bot)|n \in N\}$$

STRICT PARTIAL ORDERS

A *strict partial order* is a relation $<$ acting on a set S, which satisfies

$$(x < y) \wedge (y < z) \Longrightarrow x < z$$

$$x < y \Longrightarrow \neg(y < x)$$

We can always construct a strict partial order from a partial order by

$$x < y \Longleftrightarrow (x \leq y) \wedge (x \neq y)$$

In addition, we can always construct a partial order from a strict partial order by

$$x \leq y \Longleftrightarrow (x < y) \vee (x = y)$$

We say that S is *linearly ordered* if for any $x, y \in S$, exactly one of $x < y, y < x$, or $x = y$ holds.

Appendix B
GRAPHS AND DIGRAPHS

In this thesis, we make frequent use of *graphs* to represent various properties of networks of processes. We adopt the terminology of [Wilson 1985].

A *graph* G is defined to be a pair $(V(G), E(G))$, where $V(G)$ is a non-empty finite set of elements called *vertices* and $A(G)$ is a finite *family* of *unordered* pairs of elements of $V(G)$ called *edges*. (A family is a collection of elements like a set, except that an element may occur more than once; *e.g.*, $\{a, b, c\}$ is a set, but (a, a, c, b, a, c) is a family.)

A *digraph* D is defined to be a pair $(V(D), A(D))$, where $V(D)$ is a non-empty finite set of elements called *vertices* and $A(D)$ is a finite family of *ordered* pairs of elements of $V(D)$ called *arcs*.

A graph (or digraph) is *simple* if there are no duplicate edges (or arcs) uv and no 'loops' uu.

Figure B.1: A Graph

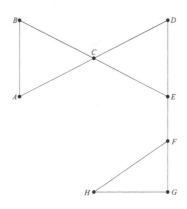

A *walk* in a graph (or digraph) is a finite sequence of edges (or arcs) of the form

$$\langle v_0 v_1, v_1 v_2, \ldots, v_{m-1} v_m \rangle$$

A walk in which all the edges (or arcs) are distinct is called a *trail*; if, in addition, the vertices $v_0, v_1, \ldots, v_m$ are distinct (except, possibly, $v_0 = v_m$), then the trail is called a *path*. A path or trail is *closed* if $v_0 = v_m$. A closed path is called a *circuit*.

The simple graph

$$(\{A, B, C, D, E, F, G, H\}, (AB, BC, CD, DE, EC, CA, EF, FH, GH, FG))$$

is illustrated in Figure B.1. Here, the sequence $\langle AB, BC, CA \rangle$ is both a closed trail and a circuit; the sequence $\langle AB, BC, CD, DE, EC, CA \rangle$ is a closed trail but not a circuit.

A graph with no circuit is known as a *tree*. If D is a digraph, the graph obtained from D by replacing each arc by a corresponding edge is called the *underlying graph* of D. A *directed tree* is a digraph of which the underlying graph is a tree.

A graph is *connected* if there exists a path between any two vertices. The vertices of a disconnected graph may be partitioned into *connected components* such that two vertices are in the same connected component if, and only if, there exists a path between them.

A graph is said to have a *separation vertex* v (sometimes called an *articulation point*) if there exist vertices a and b, where $a \neq v$ and $b \neq v$ and all paths connecting a and b pass through v. In the graph of Figure B.1, the separation vertices are $C, E,$ and F. A graph that has a separation vertex is called *separable*, and one that has none is called *non-separable*.

Let $V' \subseteq V(G)$. If the induced subgraph $G'(V', E')$ (where E' is the set of edges of G which connect vertices of V') is connected, non-separable and for every larger $V'', V' \subset V'' \subseteq V$, the induced subgraph $G''(V'', E'')$ is separable, we say that V' is a *non-separable component* of G. In Figure B.1, the non-separable components are $\{A, B, C\}, \{C, D, E\}, \{E, F\},$ and $\{F, G, H\}$.

A *disconnecting edge* of a graph is an edge, the removal of which increases by one the number of connected components. This is also known as a *bridge*. If all the disconnecting edges of a graph are removed, the residual connected components are known as *essential components* of the original graph. The graph illustrated in Figure B.1 has a single disconnecting edge, EF. Its essential components are $\{A, B, C, D, E\}$ and $\{F, G, H\}$.

A digraph is *strongly connected* if, for any two vertices u and v, there exists a path from u to v and also from v to u. The vertices of a digraph that are not strongly connected may be partitioned into *strongly connected components* using the equivalence relation ~, where $u \sim v$ means that there is a path from u to v and also from v to u.

Suppose that the vertex set of a graph (or digraph) G can be partitioned into two subsets, V_1 and V_2, such that no edge (arc) joins two elements from the same subset. We say that G is *bipartite*.

We denote by $G \backslash e$ the graph (digraph) obtained by removing an edge (arc) vw and combining vertices v and w into a single vertex (if they are distinct). This is known as an *edge contraction*. A succession of edge contractions is called a *contraction*.

THE DEPTH-FIRST SEARCH ALGORITHM

The Depth-First Search technique is a method for scanning the edges (or arcs) of a finite graph (or digraph), which is widely recognised as a powerful technique. It is used by Deadlock Checker in a variety of situations either to perform analysis of transition systems or to establish global properties of networks, such as the absence of circuits. The algorithm involves constructing a walk that traverses each edge or arc exactly once in either direction.

The algorithms given here are based on those in [Even 1979], where proofs of correctness are to be found.

DFS for Graphs
For a (possibly disconnected) graph, the algorithm proceeds as follows. Consider the graph $G = (V(G), E(G))$.

1. Set up two arrays, indexed by vertices of $V(G)$: an array of vertices called *father* and an array of integers called *order*. Also, set up a Boolean array called *used*, indexed by edges of $E(G)$. Set each element of *used* to be *false*, each element of *father* to be 'undefined', and each element of order to be 0. Also, set $i := 0$ and $v := s$ (s is the vertex we choose to start from).
2. Set $i := i + 1$ and $order(v) := i$
3. If there are no unused edges incident with v, then go to step 5
4. Choose an unused edge $v \xrightarrow{e} u$. Set $used\ (e) := true$. If *order* $(u) \neq 0$, go to step 3. Otherwise, first set *father* $(u) := v$, $v := u$ and then go to step 2.
5. If *father* (v) is defined, then set $v := father(v)$ and go to step 3.
6. (*father* (v) is undefined). If there is a vertex u for which *order* $(u) = 0$, then set $v := u$ and go to step 2.
7. (All the vertices have been scanned) Halt.

If we assume a constant time for array lookup, then this algorithm can be implemented in linear time. (To implement step 6 efficiently, it actually requires maintaining a linked list of those vertices that have not yet been visited.)

DFS for Digraphs

For a (possibly disconnected) digraph, the DFS algorithm is very similar. Consider the digraph $D = (V(D), A(D))$.

1. Set up two arrays, indexed by vertices of $V(D)$: an array of vertices called *father* and an array of integers called *order*. Also, set up a Boolean array called *used*, indexed by arcs of $A(D)$. Set each element of *used* to be *false*, each element of *father* to be 'undefined', and each element of *order* to be 0. Also, set $i := 0$ and $v := s$ (s is the vertex we choose to start from).
2. Set $i := i + 1$ and $order(v) := i$
3. If there are no unused arcs outgoing from v, then go to step 5
4. Choose an unused arc $v \xrightarrow{a} u$. Set u $used(a) := true$. If $order(u) \neq 0$, go to step 3. Otherwise, first set $father(u) := v, v := u$ and then go to step 2.
5. If $father(v)$ is defined, then set $v := father(v)$ and go to step 3.
6. ($father(v)$ is undefined). If there is a vertex u for which $order(u) = 0$, then set $v := u$ and go to step 2.
7. (All the vertices have been scanned) Halt.

Checking for Circuit-Freedom of a Digraph

The above algorithm is modified to check for the presence of a circuit in D by maintaining a Boolean array, indexed by $V(D)$, to represent which vertices belong to the current *search path*. The digraph has no circuit only if, at step 4, no vertex u is ever found that lies on the current search path.

Finding Non-Separable Components of a Graph

Consider the graph $G = (V(G), E(G))$.

1. Set up three arrays, indexed by vertices of (G) : an array of vertices called *father* and two arrays of integers called *order* and *low*. Also, set up a Boolean array called used, indexed by edges of $E(G)$, and an initially empty stack of vertices, S. Set each element of *used* to be *false*, each element of *father* to be 'undefined', and each element of *order* to be 0. Also, set $i := 0$ and $v := v_0 := s$ (s is the vertex we choose to start from).
2. Set $i := i + 1, order(v) := i, low(v) := i$. Put v on S.
3. If there are no unused edges incident with v, then go to step 5

4. Choose an unused edge $v \xrightarrow{e} u$. Set $used(e) := true$. If $order(u) \neq 0$, then set

$$low(v) := \text{Min}(low(v), order(u))$$

and go to step 3. Otherwise, first set $father\ (u) := v, v := u$ and then go to step 2.

5. If $father\ (v)$ is undefined or $father\ (v) = v_0$, go to step 9.

6. ($father\ (v) \neq v_0$) If $low(v) < order(father(v))$, then set

$$low(father(v)) := \text{Min}(low(father(v)), low(v))$$

and go to step 8.

7. $(low(v) \geq order(father(v)))father(v)$ is a separation vertex. All the vertices from S down to and including v are now removed; together with $father\ (v)$, they form a non-separable component.

8. Set $v := father(v)$ and go to step 3.

9. All vertices on S down to and including v are now removed. Together with v_0, they form a non-separable component.

10. If v_0 still has unused incident edges, then go to step 12.

11. If there is a vertex u such that $order(u) = 0$, then set $v := v_0 := u$ and go to step 2, otherwise halt.

12. Vertex v_0 is a separation vertex. Let $v := v_0$ and go to step 4.

Finding Disconnecting Edges of a Simple Graph

The disconnecting edges of a simple graph are equivalent to its non-separable components of size two. Hence, we may find the disconnecting edges of a simple graph, such as a network communication graph, using the algorithm for non-separable components.

Finding Strongly Connected Components of a Digraph

Consider the digraph $D = (V(D), A(D))$.

1. Set up three arrays, indexed by vertices of $V(D)$: an array of vertices called $father$ and two arrays of integers called order and low. Also, set up a Boolean array called $used$, indexed by arcs of $A(D)$. Create an initially empty stack of vertices S. Set each element of $used$ to be $false$, each element of $father$ to be 'undefined', and each element of $order$ to be 0. Also, set $i := 0$ and $v := s$ (s is the vertex we choose to start from).

2. Set $i := i + 1, order(v) := i$ and $low(v) := i$. Put v on S.

3. If there are no unused arcs outgoing from v, then go to step 7.

4. Choose an unused arc $v \xrightarrow{a} u$. Set $used(a) := true$. If $order(u) = 0$, set $father\ (u) := v, v := u$ and then go to step 2.

149

5. If $order(u) > order(v)$, go straight back to step 3. Otherwise, if u is not on S (u and v do no belong to the same component), go to step 3.
6. ($order(u) < order(v)$ and both vertices are in the same component.) Set

$$low(v) := \text{Min}(low(v), order(u))$$

and go to step 3.
7. If $low(v) = order(v)$, then delete all vertices from S down to and including v; these vertices form a component.
8. If $father(v)$ is defined, then set

$$low(father(v)) := \text{Min}(low(father(v)), low(v))$$
$$v := father(v)$$

and go to step 3.
9. ($father(v)$ is undefined.) If there is a vertex u for which $order(u) = 0$, then let $v := u$ and go to step 2.
10. (All the vertices have been scanned.) Halt.

Selecting Arcs from a Digraph Lying on a Circuit

We may use the above technique to find all the arcs in a digraph that lie on a circuit. (This is required for the CSDD algorithm of Deadlock Checker.) First, we partition the vertices of the digraph into strongly connected components, as described above. During the analysis, a partition number $N(v)$ is assigned to each vertex v. We then scan through the arcs uv of the graph, removing any where $N(u) \neq N(v)$. It may be easily shown that those arcs that remain are exactly those that lie on a circuit in V.

www.ingramcontent.com/pod-product-compliance
Lightning Source LLC
La Vergne TN
LVHW022346060326
832902LV00022B/4282